DOG PADDLING WITH TINY

A Guide To Kayaking With A Dog

By Lou Racine

Copyright © 2015 Lou Racine

All rights reserved.

No part of this publication may be reproduced in any form or by any means, including scanning, copying, photocopying, or any other means without prior specific written permission of the author and copyright holder.

ISBN-10: 1502849046
ISBN-13: **978-1502849045**

DEDICATION

With more love and appreciation than words could ever say, I dedicate this book

To

Cecil Grimes, Jr.

&

In Loving Memory of my son, Gary.

Gary Michael Lambert, Jr.
1981 - 2000

CONTENTS

Acknowledgements ………………………………… i

Disclaimer …………………………………............ 11

1. Introduction …………………………............…... 7

2. Should Every Dog Go Kayaking? …………….. 13

3. What Is Required …………………………..…… 19

4. What Should I Bring? …………………………... 25

5. What Kayak Is Best? ……………………………. 31

6. The Training Process …………………………….. 35

7. Problem Solving ………………………………… 47

8. Tips & Inspiration ……………………………….. 65

9. Resources ………………………………............... 74

Tiny's Favorite Dog Biscuit Recipe ……………… 76

About the Author ……………………………......... 77

ACKNOWLEDGEMENTS

Thank you Cec. This book would not have been possible without your support and encouragement. Words cannot express my gratitude. You've stood with me through the worst and best of times...and told me countless times to "write that book!" I will always grow, love, and laugh within the light of your smile.

I would also like to thank my younger brother Andy for being my big brother growing up and for always looking out for me. Not to mention the countless hours that you spent listening to me go on, and on, and on, about my dreams. You not only encouraged me to dream big, you encouraged me to believe dreams do come true. Thank you bro.

A special thank you to my friend, Mary Happel, for introducing me to kayaking with dogs! We have enjoyed kayaking with Mary and her dogs and look forward to paddling with them again after the spring thaw! *Woof!*

Mom, thank you for never saying no when I continue to ask, "Can you proof read just one more…?"

1 INTRODUCTION

Tiny chillin' on Beach Pond in Voluntown, Connecticut, USA

Hi, my name is Lou and our dog's name is Tiny (Tine Tine). I am excited that you, like so many others, are considering kayaking with a dog and I would like to thank you for choosing my book.

Bringing a dog out on the water in a kayak is an exciting experience! Our dog, Tiny, jumps up and down the moment he sees the kayaking equipment being handled and I've been told that he sulks for hours if he's left behind! Tiny is usually involved in kayaking at least once a week during the season. He enjoys lounging on deck, as well as, seeing and interacting with other dogs and animals…and the smell of barbeque; but, I like to think that he enjoys being with me even more!

Tiny is occasionally disappointed when he has to stay home! I'm sure you know what I mean; to those small dogs, nothing is too big or too dangerous! But, the reality is that every kayaking experience isn't safe for our little guy. I have to pick and choose his adventures.

Experiencing his transformation from a dog who once thought he could walk on lily pads to a seasoned pro has been exciting! Just the other day, I was maneuvering my kayak through twigs and brush, sometimes grabbing and pulling on the next branch in reach. I watched Tiny's tail wagging ahead of me as he ducked, twisted, turned, and weaved through the obstacles like a Matrix Ninja dodging bullets. Before I even stopped the kayak, Tiny had turned towards the beaver hut, giving it a once over, as if he knew it was our sole reason for our fancy maneuvers through the brush. Our Tine Tine got what it was all about and was enjoying our quest!

Before we get started, I would like to say a little about myself. I am an avid paddler, kayaking 1 - 3 times a week, weather and time permitting. I began kayaking as a kid, and I've used a variety of different kayaks, including some home-made kayaks when I was a teenager. My current kayak is a Heritage Feather-Lite Angler which is great for my purposes and for our dog. I have a life-time of experience with both kayaks and dogs, and paddling in a variety of situations, including rivers, lakes, ponds, and salt marshes; rivers are my favorite. I have a college degree and I am also a blogger; you can go to my website, KayakingCTwithLou.com, and watch videos and read information about kayaking, hiking, and Connecticut kayaking sites and boat launches.

I have taught and helped wild and domesticated animals since I was a kid and I enjoy teaching animals to do unusual tricks. You can watch our dog, Candy, turn the door knob and open our front door in one of my many informational online horse videos. I taught my horse, Chap, to throw a partially deflated basketball back to me with precision accuracy. He does other tricks like right a barrel with his nose, flap his lips around (pretend talking), play catch, bob for apples, pretend to count, pretend to take a drink, and more... There are many online videos showing how I taught my horse, donkey, and dog to do various tricks.

More importantly, I have taught in a manner that teaches animals the essential tools of learning to communicate and interact with humans and they surprise me every day. *Watch my horse adjust the camera in this video on my You Tube channel, Horses Can Think:*
https://www.youtube.com/watch?v=gW-UGYL21YI

Of course, the horse in this video didn't know what the camera does; however, I believe he had seen it adjusted enough times that he knew it should be facing the action, LOL! I believe that teaching an animal in the way that I teach animals, encourages them to think and learn independent of the training. They learn to learn! Working with animals over the years, it has become apparent to me that animals can think at a higher level than many people believe possible!

Tiny on deck, approaching Butts Bridge on the Quinnebaug River in Canterbury, CT.

Teaching animals is easiest when the person is knowledgeable of what they're doing, and can relax and recognize the fun in it, and relay that fun to the animal. At the same time the person must be on guard, keeping a watchful eye on the situation, adjusting for surprises, and making an effort to keep the situation safe for all involved; yes, it's a bit of a juggling act, but with teaching comes with responsibility.

Never loose sight of the fun! Many times I see people try, and fail, to teach animals because they get so caught up in the process and in thinking that everything has to be done perfectly every time. Your dog is not expecting perfection and will adjust to the mistakes that you might make, so relax and have fun with it! View mistakes as opportunities to learn and grow! Your dog might surprise you and teach you something that will help you become an even better teacher and paddler!

Please read this book in its entirety and then talk with your vet and dog trainer about kayaking with your dog before introducing your dog to the kayaking experience. If after reading this complete book, you feel you won't be able to safely do the things in it, please find a local dog trainer or kayaking instructor who can help you. If after reading this complete book, you have a specific question, please feel free to email me at KayakingCTwithLou@paddlingCT.com and I'll try to answer specific questions time permitting.

    Your input is valuable to me. If you like this book, please take a few moments to write a nice review for it at the site on which you purchased it. Your review is valuable because it will help others know that it's a good read and will help promote the book. Promoting and selling the book would help me allot more "work time" to writing books. If you disliked it, please email me at *KayakingCTwithLou@paddingCT.com* and let me know why so that I can improve it. I appreciate your input. Thank you.

DISCLAIMER:

This book is for informational purposes only and it is not meant to replace instruction with a professional kayak instructor and/or professional dog trainer. I cannot see your dog's level of training, your level of understanding, the specific situations in which you will be kayaking, or the specific equipment that you might use, so I cannot offer specific advice for you and your dog. The content of this book is general information that I think might be useful and helpful to dog owners who wish to kayak with their dogs.

All readers are advised to seek help from local competent professionals in the dog training and kayaking field before bringing a dog out on the water for the first time. I have a life-time of experience training animals and kayaking; however, I am not a professional dog trainer, nor am I a professional kayak instructor.

You must read the information presented and make your own judgment regarding what you think will, or will not, be safe and what is best for you and your dog. There are risks involved in both kayaking and working with dogs; if you choose to do the activities in this book, do so at your own risk. It is very important that you read the entire book and not skip around, thus missing important aspects of the process.

2 SHOULD EVERY DOG GO KAYAKING?

Before I get into the actual process, I would like to thank you for picking up my book. Many of your questions should be answered in the following question and answer section of the book, making you better prepared to read about the actual teaching process that I have used. Please do not skip this section.

Tiny on deck under the bridge at Glasgo Pond, Glasgo, Connecticut, USA

WHAT ABOUT SIZE?

The size, weight, and personality of a dog play an important role in deciding whether a dog should be included in kayaking activities. It's been my experience that small to small/medium size dogs with low-key personalities usually make great paddling companions. These smaller dogs can easily and quietly reposition themselves, moving between the deck and inside the cockpit without crowding, distracting, and/or obstructing the paddler.

There are a variety of riding preferences among dogs; however, once a dog chooses their style, they seem to stick with it. I know a poodle that rides on deck and will move from one deck to another, and do so quietly and with great confidence, if the kayaks are parked close together. Our dog Tiny moves back and forth from cockpit to deck, but stays on deck most of the time, and two other dogs that kayak with us choose to only stay inside the cockpit.

Always safety first! Be certain that having a dog in the kayak with you isn't going to hinder your ability to maneuver the kayak and that you can safely exit the kayak in an emergency situation! I strongly advise against squeezing a medium to large dog inside a sit-in type kayak with a paddler. For example, this could create a dangerous situation where the dog might cause the kayak to flip or both owner and dog might become stuck inside if the kayak were to flip; Not to mention, it would become very uncomfortable for both paddler and dog.

I have not tried paddling with a dog on a sit-on type kayak, but I have seen medium size dogs seeming to be quite comfy sitting on them with their owners. Canoes and 2-seater kayaks also might be better suited for medium size dogs.

DOES THE DOG'S PERSONALITY MATTER?

Tiny on the river just north of Beachdale Pond in Voluntown, Connecticut, USA.

Sure, a calm quiet personality would probably be the easiest dog to have along on a kayaking trip if all you are considering is the time and individual attention that will be required for the dog during these trips. Other personality types might require more initial training; however, they might be a bit more fun in the long run!

Of course, it's always great fun to have along a dog that makes you laugh! Our dog Tine Tine is such a dog. Sometimes we just know something silly is going to happen! Like when he gets so determined to catch that darn horse fly! He quickly forgets he's on deck and lands in the drink, bobbing around like a fishing bobber waiting to be air-lifted to the deck again!

CAN A DOG WITH A DISABILITY GO KAYAKING?

If a dog is interested and enthusiastic about being included in any safe appropriate activity with you, it is often worth the effort to find a way to include them. Ask your vet and dog trainer if kayaking would be a safe activity for your dog before taking it out on the water!

Our dog, Shana, used a doggy wheel chair for the last months of her life because she still wanted to go go go even though her hind legs gave up on her. Some common sense must be used;

I would NEVER put such a dog in a kayak; but I would include, and did include, that dog in camping trips and short hikes.

Our dog, Tiny loves kayaking; however, he is old and has some slight and infrequent instability issues, but walks, runs, and swims without issue. His age related special needs meant that I had to make adjustments to my kayak so that he could ride safely and confidently on the water with us. I tried several different set-ups on the deck of my kayak before arriving at the one that worked and was easy to add and remove. Most healthy dogs, that I've interacted with, have only needed something similar to a removable piece of indoor/outdoor mat on the deck. *More info regarding the deck mat in Chapter 4.*

After much trial and error, I created a "dog bed" type situation on the deck of my kayak for Tiny. This "deck bed" addressed his infrequent momentary imbalances and his age related need to rest more often. The sides of our dog's deck bed were made by inserting pool noodles into sewn upholstery fabric; this creates the bumper sides seen in the photo below. I can remove or include the "deck bed" in only 2 minutes and I can also easily remove the pool noodles and wash the bed in the washer and dryer!

If you look closely at the photo below, you can see the bungee cords that run from the back of my kayak, through the cup holders and through holes in the dog bed, which then attach to the kayak cord hold-downs under the material. This is what holds the bed in place. It is also clipped in place at the carry handle hold-down in front This is an early photo; I later added a piece of indoor-outdoor carpet to the bottom to give it more stability and to prevent the fabric from becoming worn and ruined. *Note: cup holders are slightly askew because we were maneuvering tight spaces in this situation so I took my dog into the kayak and pulled the cup holders inside as well.*

Photo of the dog bed on deck as we squeezed through weeds and grass on the Pachaug River in Voluntown, Connecticut, USA.

Ask yourself, would you leave your best human friend home because they had a disability or would you first try to help them safely join you? Please make that same decision when you have a dog with a disability. Always keep safety and common sense in mind. For example, I would NEVER put a dog that couldn't use its legs in a kayak; however, I would consider putting a dog with three legs that could balance, walk, run, and swim in one with modifications to aid the dog if the dog's owner, vet, and trainer agreed it would be safe to do so!

Again, it's up to you to decide what is or isn't safe for you and your dog! Always check with your vet and trainer before putting any dog in a kayak; but, this is especially important when a dog has a known disability. If you can't find a safe way to include your dog, don't beat yourself up--just find another activity that the two of you can enjoy together and feel good about having tried! Your dog appreciates your efforts on its behalf!

CAN A DOG BE ON BOARD IF THE PADDLER IS FISHING?

A dog should be introduced to the kayaking process and have many trips under its collar, so to speak, before being introduced to things like fishing from a kayak. When you do introduce the experienced dog to kayak fishing, consider things like a dog's natural tendency to retrieve things. I've seen dogs jump in the water and try to retrieve a cast line with a fishing bobber on it! LOL! I've seen a dog jump in to retrieve a cast bobber from another boat!

I fished a lot when I was younger, but no longer fish, so our current dog, Tiny, is not directly involved in this activity; however, we sometimes go out with other paddlers who fish and other paddlers who have dogs onboard while they fish.

WHAT IF MY DOG HATES KAYAKING?

This is a valid and important question, but don't be too quick to try and answer it! First, give your dog several opportunities to get out on the water in a variety of safe and appropriate situations and vary the experiences if possible. Most dogs enjoy being with their owners and your dog will likely want to be with you once it accepts floating around on a seemingly unpredictable moving object!

If your dog falls in the water, don't count that outing as one of the "several opportunities" mentioned above. You want the dog to have experienced several positive outings before trying to assess whether your dog likes it or not. Think about yourself for a moment. Say you played golf for the first time and you lost the ball, hit every sand and water trap, and never got the ball in the hole your first time out! You might think you hate golf; however, if you were to go out again on an easier course and you were more relaxed, you might begin to have fun. Give your dog these experiences and time to adjust and learn as well.

Some dogs who seem to initially dislike the kayaking experience, don't hate kayaking, they dislike what happens when they go kayaking. Again, consider yourself for a moment; you can go kayaking with one friend and have a blast and then go to the same location with another person and be bored out of your skull!

Try to understand that our dog's interests are different from our own! Our dogs don't care what lure is being tried out or how pretty the foliage might be! Dogs are interested in adventure and stimulating sights, sounds and smells--and being with us! The smell of barbeque, the sound of distant barking, and the appearance of animals, people, and new smells all invite our dogs to more thoroughly enjoy the experience.

Tiny on deck, checking out a heron (left) just before dark.

Create a kayaking experience that blends things you want and like to do with experiences that would be liked and appreciated by your dog. Such as stopping at least once every trip to explore a little on shore. Paddle close to a turtle so your dog can watch it plop into the water. Follow some ducks! Let it smell and investigate. Use your knowledge of your dog and your creative imagination to make your kayaking trips fun for you and your dog and give the dog time to learn what it's all about before you ask yourself, "What if my dog hates kayaking?"

3 WHAT IS REQUIRED?

Did you say, "Let's go?"

ARE DOGS REQUIRED TO WEAR LIFE JACKETS?

Check the regulations in your state to see if dogs are required to wear life jackets and act accordingly. Even if your state does not require that your dog wear a life jacket, I suggest that you consider this safety option. Suppose you flip your kayak and you can't get to your dog right away; the upset and recovery period will likely be less stressful if you can see your dog safely floating near you and its wrapped in the safety of its own life jacket!

Cec purchased our dog's life jacket online, but some of the larger pet stores also carry them. Be certain the jacket fits and has been tested on the dog prior to using it while kayaking. An ill-fitting jacket can be worse than no jacket at all! A dog can get caught up in an ill-fit or torn jacket, hindering its ability to swim and float correctly, causing the dog anxiety, possible injury, and even death.

The life jacket should fit snug, but not tight and the end of the jacket should not extend farther than just before the dogs tail area; the front of the jacket shouldn't be riding up into the dog's chin or down too low--right across the mid-chest area is perfect. Be sure that when you test the jacket on the dog, that the dog doesn't catch its feet in the strap that goes across the front while swimming in it; this could be a sign of an ill-fitting piece of equipment.

I would also put the jacketed dog into the water on its side and make sure that the jacket rights the dog. The dog should be brought to the upright position with its nose safely clear of the water. Please don't hold the dog on its side for a long length of time; if it's willing, just tip it to the side enough to release it and see that the jacket will right the dog.

A life jacket that is riding up on one side is a sure sign that something needs to be corrected! The following photo shows Tiny's life jacket riding up on the far side and down on the side closest to the camera. In this case, I have a heavy leash and clasp attached directly to the jacket; if he pulls sharply on the leash, it pulls the jacket down on that side. If I attach the leash to something other than the jacket, this won't happen. This doesn't usually happen when I use the lighter retractable leash that flexes in and out because the retractable leash, when set to flex, never comes to an abrupt stop so it doesn't pull on the jacket *(second photo below)*. However, the retractable leash has its shortcomings as well. I find he gets tangled in it easier than the traditional leash.

(Above) Tiny's jacket pulled down on Beach Pond in Voluntown, Connecticut, USA.

(Above) Tiny with retractable leash on deck at the Hampton Reservoir in Hampton, Connecticut, USA.

Also take your jacketed dog for at least a few walks to be sure the dog can pee without peeing all over the jacket and ensure that the jacket doesn't hinder its movement. If the dog's movements are obstructed while walking, it's very likely the jacket will also hinder it's movement while swimming. You might be chuckling over the pee on the jacket aspect, but believe me, the last thing you want is your dog peeing on its life jacket and hopping back in the kayak with you! Been there, smelled that! Also having to remove the dog's jacket every time it needs to pee will get old very fast.

I once put our dog's life jacket on him and left it loose because we were hanging about and I didn't want him to get overheated waiting on us. Of course, he peed and the pee went inside the jacket because it was hanging down too low. I tried to clean him and the jacket as best I could, without soaking either of them; but, the reality was that I smelled pee for the entire afternoon as he stood in front of me on deck on a hot afternoon!

If you purchase a life jacket in a pet store, ask for assistance in picking the proper jacket and bring the dog with you. Make sure you know what the return policy is before you test a life jacket on your dog; sometimes you can't return an ill-fitting jacket if its been tried on the dog in water, even if its clean clear water.

It might be a bit challenging to find the proper jacket for some dogs, such as an over-weight dog, under-weight dog, or some mixed breeds. Our dog, Tiny for example has a deep chest but narrows sharply after the rib cage. For unusual situations like this, I would recommend that you consult a local professional that could help you.

ARE DOGS REQUIRED TO WEAR A LEASH?

Please consider having the dog wear a dog harness and not a dog collar. I don't like things around the neck of a dog when it's possible that the kayak could flip and/or the dog could fall out and get hung up on something. Even if a leash is not attached to the dog's collar, the collar itself can still get caught on something in the water if the dog falls or jumps in. In this situation, the collar could become a noose around the dog's neck! For this reason, our dog wears a harness and not a collar.

Check your local leash laws for your state and local area. The same leash laws that apply to walking your dog in public will most likely apply. Your local dog warden should be able to help you obtain this information. Keep in mind that you are responsible for any damage and/or injury inflicted upon others and their property by your dog while your dog is in public whether you're on the water or on shore.

My dog is leashed at all times, with the leash attached to the middle back area of the life jacket (similar to a dog harness). I loop the end of the leash over my wrist with the leash going under the paddle or I clip it to my life jacket or my key loop. This is something you will have to play around with and see what is safe, comfortable, and works best for you and your dog.

I do have friends who do not leash their dogs while kayaking. However, I find that it's much easier for me to guide my dog back to the kayak if he's fallen or jumped in while wearing a leash. I can also pull my dog to the surface faster if he falls in; even wearing a life jacket, he momentarily goes under when he first falls into the water. DO NOT secure the leash to the paddle or the kayak! If the kayak flips or the dog falls out, and the dog is attached to the kayak, it could become injured or trapped.

Our dog is so accustomed to kayaking that he will do things like ask to pee as if he were going to the front door of our house and asking to go outside; I can then pull up to the shore and remain in the kayak while I wait for him to exit, pee, and return to the deck! I use a retractable leash to keep him from exploring too far and getting caught in bushes, etc. This type of behavior comes with patience, time, and teaching the dog what is expected in a kind and considerate manner <u>over time</u>.

I usually have a standard leash on my dog while he's in the kayak and I switch to the retractable leash when he goes ashore to pee. The standard leash is too short for this peeing ritual and he gets tangled in the retractable leash if I leave it on him while he's in the kayak. I've been experimenting with ways to alter the retractable leash to make it better suited for my dog's needs and will update this progress on my website, KayakingCTwithLou.com. You can go to my website and subscribe to our quarterly newsletter on the right side of the screen and receive updates about things like this as well as other kayaking information, CT site reviews, new book releases, etc.

Some state parks and other kayaking locations will require leashes and in some cases forbid dogs in certain areas; some places will exclude dogs from the entire park. Check online before you head out to a location and/or read signs posted at the launch areas and entrances to parks. Even though we might not like the idea of our dogs being excluded from certain parks and areas, we should realize that its done with the intent to protect the well-being of the general public and also our dogs.

Note: regulations might vary from salt water to fresh water situations; however, I would NEVER take a dog out on the ocean in a kayak and I DO NOT recommend doing it!

SERIOUSLY, WHAT ABOUT THE FUN?

Hopefully, all of you agree that fun is a requirement! I believe you would; however, at the same time, I know that there are at least two groups of readers who are also feeling some apprehension as they deliver their weak and uncertain "yes."

There is one group of paddlers who will, by no fault of their own, make this experience into tedious and boring training sessions, trying to create the perfect lessons, the perfect situation, the perfect outcome, and the perfect photos and videos. They can't help it; that's how they are. I used to be like this, so I can talk quite freely and honestly about how giving up on the *idea of creating perfection and being in total control* dramatically changed my life. Trust me, you don't know what true fun is until you do!

If you see yourself in any part of the above paragraphs, I'm here to tell you that you can't experience that all consuming depth of fun and excitement that comes with experiencing your dog's first ride if you're hogging all the control and trying to make everything just oh so perfect! To these people, I say, "Let go, and let your dog teach you how!"

That's right, if you're an experienced kayaker and you've prepared and learned all you can about paddling with a dog, and you've got the kayak and necessary equipment, and done all the necessary preparation, give up on your *belief in perfection and absolute control* and let your dog show you how it's done!

When you arrive at the kayaking destination, let your dog take control by letting Skippy choose what happens next. You've picked a safe area in your pre-check visits, so if your dog chooses to take a walk first, take a walk. If your dog wants to visit other paddlers on the shore, let it, as long as the paddlers are open to your dog's advances; your dog just might introduce you to someone who might help relieve some of your nervous energy. If your dog wants to just sit and look at the water, do that.

When your dog finally looks to you with an expression that asks, "*well*, is that it? What's next?" get the kayak and all of your equipment and proceed only when your dog is ready. Once on the water, continue to look to your dog to tell you what should happen next. At first, this will seem awkward and not much fun; but, trust me, this is your gateway to more fun than you've probably experienced in a long time! Yes, you need to plan a day trip. It probably won't take all day; but, pack lunches and prepare for a long fun day with your dog!

Try not to worry about what others might think if....happens. The people around you are more preoccupied with their own personal experiences than yours. Even the people who are kayaking with you are going to be more preoccupied with their own experience than in all the minute details of what you're doing or not doing. I find that, many times, people bring my attention to their missteps by saying something about them. "Oh shit, why did I do that?" will quickly make everyone look at your misstep! So don't feel like you have to justify and verbalize every mistake; quietly move on, and they might not even notice!

If someone chuckles over one of your obvious missteps, consider that they are most likely chuckling because they are recalling some of their own early experiences and thinking, "Been there, done that!" And remember that you can't please and impress everyone; there will always be people who like what you do and those who don't.

Tiny on deck, approaching Middle Reservoir under Rte 101 in East Killingly CT, USA

If you fit into the second category and you're worried and maybe even a bit anxious *(maybe very anxious)*, I'm with ya, and I understand where you're coming from! I know what you're going through because after I lost my 18 year old son in a car accident several years ago, I went through a rather long period of time where I didn't do things like kayaking, hiking, etc and I experienced panic attacks and worried about every little minute thing! The compounded worry and anxiety eventually escalated to a point where I no longer had a choice--it had to be dealt with.

NOTE: Nothing that I'm about to say here, is meant to replace counseling or professional help; if you feel overwhelmed by anxiety and/or depression, please get professional help. At the same time, I want you to realize you're not alone!

For those of you who very much want to follow through and participate in this new experience with your dog, but at the same time are experiencing worry and anxiety, there is hope! After losing my son, I had no sense of identity and I had no idea what I wanted to do; I was just existing and doing a very poor version of it. I had been a mother for 18 years and then found myself thinking, who was I, if not a mother?

It will be tough for people who have not experienced this to understand, but I no longer had any idea regarding what I liked or wanted to do. A lifetime of identity, hobbies, dreams, and goals had been wiped away--in a way, who I was died too.

I implemented many strategies that I learned through life experiences and by reading, watching videos, and talking with others dealing with these issues. It might seem a bit odd, but I felt most scared when I felt myself start to heal!

I don't want to stray too far off topic, so I'll keep this simple; I might, at a later time, write about my recovery from anxiety and depression. If you visit my website, KayakingCTwithLou.com, and subscribe to my quarterly email newsletter on the right side of the screen, you will be kept informed of new book releases as well as other helpful kayaking information.

One day, after my long quest for knowledge and the experimentation and implementation of many techniques, I asked myself this question, "If I could do anything, right now, what would it be?" I asked myself this over and over and kept a journal of the answers. After about a month of doing this, I looked at the journal and realized that 75% of the time I had written, go kayaking. Now, this 75% number doesn't mean that I liked kayaking 75% more than everything else; it means that my subconscious was bringing it to the surface 75% of the time for a very specific reason. *As Teal says, "Our minds are very helpful to the healing process if only we listen." Thank you Teal Scott/Swan for your insightful You Tube videos on this and other helpful self-help topics (You Tube Channel: Ask Teal)!*

I woke one morning knowing this was to be a day of great potential so I asked the question and acted on the answer! I went kayaking! I was drawn to Butts Bridge (Quinnebaug River boat launch area) with such intensity that I felt compelled to go there; this had the potential to be a very volatile and unpredictable experience because this is one of the most beautiful kayaking sites in the area; but, it was also tragically scarred by the loss of my son's life on Butts Bridge Road.

I won't get into all the details of this experience because this is not what this book is about, but I will say that I walked right by self-doubt, passed through all the confusion and put my kayak in the water and paddled....I paddled for hours until it got dark and I came back a changed person. It was as if I had looked back over my shoulder and said, "Hey anxiety...yeah, you too depression, don't be here when I get back!"

There were several things I did leading up to this point that brought me to that moment of great and significant change in my life; it was a long and sometimes difficult journey for me and the people closest to me. I know what I've said won't, on its own, be of significant value to people who are struggling with anxiety and want to participate in the kayaking experience with their dog. However, I want you to know that you're not alone, and that if you start working on it, it doesn't always have to be that way.

If you're feeling anxious about going out on the water for the first time with your dog, please seek help from a local well-seasoned dog trainer and/or a competent kayaking instructor and do not try to do it on your own! I also suggest that you find some very supportive people to go with you and your dog on your dog's first kayaking trips; take in the thrill and beauty around you and recharge your mind.

4 WHAT SHOULD I BRING?

Tiny falls for a tiny dog.

Tiny on deck on Bog Meadow Reservoir, looking into Middle Reservoir in E. Killingly CT

WHAT DOG-RELATED ITEMS SHOULD BE ONBOARD?

I have created a list of some items below. I also recommend that you discuss your desire to take your dog kayaking with your vet and dog trainer. They can help you create a list that includes items specific to your dog's individual needs. You could also brainstorm ideas with your friends at the dog park; after all, they know specifics about you and your dog!

In general, I find it's convenient to have a list of things that I normally bring on kayaking trips; having a list prevents me from forgetting things like binoculars, sun glasses, dog treats, etc. I have a small pack that has most of the items I normally bring so that I don't have to repack a bag every time. Our dog jumps up and down and bows, crossing both front feet when he sees that bag retrieved from its storage area.

ITEMS TO BRING:

- Recommendations from your vet/trainer that you think are appropriate for you and your dog

- Keep a laminated photo of your dog in your onboard emergency first aid kit and one in a prominent position in your wallet. These photos should be of your dog out on the water with you if possible; the dog's name and nick name should be on the back with the words, "Dog might be on-board! If this is a kayaking related emergency, please verify at…" and list your home phone, your cell, and another alternate number of someone who typically would know you're out on the water and if your dog might be with you. If something happens to you, people will typically go to the emergency kit for supplies and/or your wallet for ID. The photo being of your dog on the water with you would be the first thing that might trigger the viewer to consider looking for your dog. If they turn it over, they will know they should determine your dog's where-abouts. It's important to have both the dog's name and nick name on the back of the photos because you want them to be using the name you use to call it and not its "official" name if they call to it. *I learned this valuable tip from a hunter when I was a teenager.*

- If you plan to kayak with your dog a lot, I would suggest your dog wear a tag with your number and an additional emergency phone number on it. Tag should read, "If found contact….."

- If your kayak has an "if found" sticker on it, include in that information that a dog might be involved.

- Include your vet's phone number and the office after hours number in the first aid kit and in the pocket of your dog's life jacket, in case something happens to you, and someone else has to call the vet on your dog's behalf. Also list any allergies, special conditions and all drugs the dog might currently be taking. Also list your cell phone number and an alternate number of a friend or family member. This information should be laminated or in a sealed water-proof zip lock bag, or preserved in some other way that water won't destroy it.

- First aid kit: Check with your vet for a list of items for your individual dog.

- Dog's rabies, license, and other identifying tags should be up to date and worn by the dog.

- A mat with a grippy rubber underside for the bottom of the kayak--the dog will enjoy sitting on this mat more so than the hard cold bottom of the kayak. I use a mat that I bought for $1 at the Dollar Store. It's usually in my kayak even when our dog isn't because it absorbs any water from my feet or water splashed into the kayak from other sources. Use caution when you enter and exit the boat because this mat could slip and move; you don't want to trip and fall.

- A small light blanket. Handy in an emergency or if the dog happens to get wet and chilled. Our dog also likes to go under his when taking a nap.

- A winter dog coat or sweater in case the dog falls in the water and becomes chilled; small dogs can become momentarily chilled even in summer weather.

- Its own towel

- Bug repellent appropriate for dogs

- Small water bowl with a flat grippy bottom

- Bottled water so the dog doesn't have to drink pond or river water

- Snacks & a sealed packet of dog kibbles

- A chew toy or filled Kong toy in case the dog becomes bored

- Poop bags

- Something, such as a piece of indoor/outdoor carpeting, secured to the deck of the kayak so that the dog can have something to grip when on deck. I cut a piece of indoor/outdoor carpet to the shape and size of the deck and then cut 4 off centered slits that lined up with the hold-downs for the criss-crossing bungee cords. I rolled the piece of carpet and passed it under the criss-crossing cords back to front *(photo 1 next page)*. I then fed the carpet out under the cords to the edges of the kayak, using the cord hold-downs to hold the carpet in place *(photo 2)*. Our dog Tiny felt quit comfortable with this set up *(photo 3)* and this piece of carpet can be left on or easily removed and added as needed.

Tiny chillin' on deck at Beaver Brook Pond, trying out the new deck mat.

Bring along a very relaxed attitude:

I can quickly think of a few ways to help accomplish this before you leave your home. First, pick and wear clothing that is loose fitting and has that care-worn feeling about it; you know what I'm talking about, those items that are still in your closet because you just can't toss them out. They're still there and not replaced by something newer and more fashionable because they're comfortable and they make you feel good when you wear them. They are also items that you won't worry about ruining.

Don't wear your best clothes when you're out on the water with your dog. Your clothes will quickly down grade after the dog gets water, snacks, and mud on them or a claw gets caught on your favorite outfit; more importantly, new clothes will not be as comfy as those tried and true care worn items hiding out in your closet and drawers. I like light loose-fitting shirts and stretch shorts or sweat pants. Shorts that extend to my knees help prevent nicks and scratches from puppy toes as well as blocking over-exposure to the sun.

I like sunglasses with a yellow or yellow-based tint. I find them to be relaxing to my eyes and the view through them is crisp and bright. I absolutely hate blue tinted sunglasses; I can actually feel my eyes strain and my head start to pound. If I find myself paddling into the sun wearing yellow or yellow-based sun glasses, I can pull my visor down to rest on the top of my sun glasses and see comfortably without squinting. There are also different types of sun glasses available that can help you see into the water better.

This next point is as much a safety issue as it is one of comfort. I never wear lace-up boots or shoes in a kayak and I always wear my life jacket even if it's piping hot outside. You might occasionally catch me with my life jacket unbuckled on a scorching summer afternoon or I might take it off for a photo or to demonstrate a technique, but I never paddle without wearing a jacket.

When I was a teenager, I was out in a kayak and a friend and I were pushing and splashing each other, playing like teens often do. I lost my balance and my kayak flipped and my friend high-tailed it out of there; I suppose because he was avoiding the repercussions that he knew would follow when I righted my kayak. But I didn't right my kayak because I wasn't wearing my life jacket and I was wearing high lace up boots--my life jacket was under the deck of my over-turned kayak which was floating some distance away from me. My heavy lace up boots were tiring me out and dragging me under faster than I could get them unlaced!

I quickly came to the realization that I could possibly drown! Every time I came up for air, I held my hand in the air and yelled help, went under and tried to get the boots off. I could see some of my friends on shore, not fully understanding the severity of the situation, and laughing. I knew that I wasn't going to be able to unlace and remove the boots; but, in the seconds above water, I couldn't emphasize my distress in a convincing manner because to my friends I was an experienced kayaker. In their minds, they were thinking, she's got this; she's just trying to get one of us out there so she can retaliate for the dunk!

The last time I went under, I could feel my hand exposed to the air for what seemed like a long time, but as much as I struggled, I could barely get top-side again. I remember the water was very green and the slivers of sunlight shining into it looked like sharp knife blades; I felt surprisingly calm. Ironically, it was my friend with a disability, and the person least likely to be able to swim out to help me, who reacted first!

Since that day, I only wear water shoes or non-lace pull on/off boots to get into, and out of, a kayak. Even in the cooler months of the year, I still only wear water shoes or pull on/off boots. They're not as warm as lace up shoes and boots; in fact, they're horrible from that perspective because they have no real isolative value to them....so I take them off once I get into the kayak and store them under the deck.

If my feet do start to feel cold, I pull out a pair of comfy thick socks and/or slippers and put them on. LOL If its really cold, I've also been known to put boot insulators (without the boots) over the slippers! Socks and slippers aren't going to drag me to the bottom if I fall into cold water and they're so darn comfy out of sight under the deck! Yes, now you know my deepest-hidden cool-weather kayaking secret! LOL Socks and slippers!

In addition to clothing, bring along things that you usually enjoy when you relax, like your favorite tea or coffee. I like to bring along coffee in a preheated insulated container because drinking coffee always makes me feel relaxed.

Animals take their cues from the people around them. Have you ever heard people say that so-and-so's dog acts just like them? Well this is, in part, because animals mirror the people around them. If you're dog consistently does things that drive you nuts, take a good look at yourself and the people around you before blaming the dog!

If you're relaxed and confident, your dog is more likely to settle into the idea that kayaking is nothing to worry about more quickly than if you're uptight about the situation. Soooo, bring along a relaxed attitude and have fun!

Eagleville Lake, Coventry, Connecticut, USA

Yes, now you know my deepest-hidden cool-weather kayaking secret! LOL Slippers!

NOTE: If you've never flipped a kayak, I suggest that you have a professional kayaking instructor help you do this. Also have them teach you how to stop your kayak from flipping once you've reached the outer balancing points of your kayak. There are paddle maneuvers that can help prevent your kayak from flipping when you're approaching that point of no return--if you know what they are and know how to use them properly!

5 WHAT KAYAK IS BEST?

Tiny on deck entering the Pachaug River in Jewett City, Connecticut, USA.

The kayak should be one that is best suited for the type of kayaking that you do most! However, there are options to consider that might also be convenient for your dog. In my case, the options that are perks for me are also great options for dogs as well.

I strongly advise against taking a dog out on/in a kayak that is designed specifically for doing tricks. These kayaks are designed to roll more easily and to maneuver differently from fishing and recreational kayaks. Using kayaks that are meant for doing tricks could be dangerous and even put you and your dog's life in jeopardy.

I like a flat deck and large open cockpit like on my Heritage Feather-Lite Angler for a small to small/medium size dog because the dog can stand and balance better on the flat deck and move more freely from the deck into the spacious cockpit. The open cockpit is personally more comfortable for me because I can relax and spread out without feeling like I'm jammed into a small hole. Also, if I flip a kayak with a more open cockpit, I can exit the kayak easier and safer with my dog than if we were both more tightly compacted into a smaller area. My kayak is designed for fishing and works great for someone, like myself, who kayaks with a dog and loves photography and creating videos.

Not all dogs will move from the cockpit to the deck. Some prefer to be in/on one or the other and stay there. Our more active male Miniature Pincher moves between the two, but spends more time on deck. I have noticed what I think might be an invalidated pattern; I tend to see more male dogs preferring to be on deck vs. in the cockpit. More dogs will have to take to the water before we can say whether this is a genuine fact or just a coincidence.

I love the flat bottom on my kayak when taking photos and videos. If you watch the brief kayaking video *(link in the reference section of this book)*, you'll see that even with the dog moving around on deck, the video camera remains very steady; that is due to the flat bottom on my kayak! It is, as I mentioned earlier, one of the aspects of kayaking that was important to my kayaking experience which also assists our dog. It's not uncommon for me to take well over 100 photos, and sometimes hours of video each trip, so a steady kayak is important! Thank goodness for digital!

A flat bottom kayak like mine is less likely to rock around as the dog moves about and it is also comforting to dogs that are new to kayaking for that same reason. My kayak is positioned on the water from side to side and almost front to back on a flat bottom. I can literally stand up in this floating kayak! A flat bottom can also help the paddler when accommodating the dog and the slight imbalances the dog can create.

Dogs however will usually acclimate themselves to whatever type of bottom your kayak has, learning to balance and adjust themselves accordingly, so long as the paddler maintains good balance and control over the kayak. The exception might be very young or very old dogs with balancing issues and dogs that tend to be over-active or easily excited and distracted.

Those people who know me personally would tell you that I love my ol' Heritage kayak! You can view the many photos of our dog, Tiny, using my kayak on our site, KayakingCTwithLou.com. I do not receive any compensation for saying that I like this particular kayak; it just happens to be my personal favorite for what I do.

Hmmm...Where are the beavers?

There's not much that beats the feeling one gets, when paddling in their favorite kayak with their favorite dog--the day that pup goes pro! I experienced this myself on a very special day. I had returned to a childhood fishing spot a short while after two of my childhood friends had passed. Knowing that my two friends, and a third who had passed a few years earlier, would never return to this place made this a nostalgic and yet somber reunion with my old fishing haunt.

There was no formal boat launch. As kids we never gave much thought to shoving our boats down the embankment and scrambling into the floating kayaks, canoes, rafts, row boats, or whatever we happened to have on any given day. Everyone went. Nobody was left behind even if we had to *squeeze squeeze squeeze* everyone in.

Lowering myself into my floating kayak, I watched Tiny jump on deck from the embankment. This caused a smile to spread glowingly across my face. Usually he would wiggle his stub tail, pacing and bowing, as he waited to be air lifted to the deck. Not this day; he was feeling confident in a situation that was more awkward and challenging than he was accustomed to....and he jumped right in!

Paddling with Tiny on point, we watched for ducks, turtles...and whatever else might show itself. I took my time remembering days long since experienced; recalling a time and place where the outside stresses of our little worlds didn't matter and our personalities and friendships collided, culminating into the ultimate childhood experiences. It was such a simple time. Satisfied to dig some worms and clamor into our boats and fish, we would later start the evening fire along the shore and tell exaggerated and exciting stories of that day and days before. Still later, we would make our way safely back to our different homes in time for curfews, smelling of smoke and fish, and swearing we hadn't done what we had! Not that any of what we had done was bad; but, we weren't supposed to be out on the water or starting fires without "supervision." *Wink wink.*

I put my paddle to one side and pulled my kayak through the twigs and brush in the back of the pond, grabbing and pulling on the next branch in reach; all this effort to see if the beavers were still there. As I did this, I watched our dog on deck ducking, twisting, turning, and weaving like a

Matrix Ninja dodging bullets. Before I attempted to stop the kayak, Tiny had turned towards the beaver hut, giving it a once over, as if he knew the lodge was our sole reason for his fancy maneuvers through the brush.

It was in these few moments of time that I realized our dog had gone pro. The dog who once thought he could walk on lily pads was transformed. The dog standing on deck wagging his stub tail and checking out the beaver lodge was a grand transformation indeed--he got it. He knew what this was all about and he enjoyed it as much as I.

Tiny's stub tail wagged, stopped, wagged as he stood on point, watching and waiting to see what would happen next. Glancing back at me, he then turned back to the ducks that had just appeared in front of us, and I knew that if he were a person, that passing glance would've been a huge thumbs up! Our Tine Tine was living the dream....

6 THE TRAINING PROCESS

"Just let me at 'em! I'll get that horse fly!!!" --or end up in the drink trying!

This is a guide showing the process that I have used and is intended to supplement training, not replace training, with a professional kayak instructor and/or dog trainer. I cannot see your dog's level of training, your level of understanding, the specific situations in which you will be kayaking, or the specific equipment that you might use, so I cannot offer specific advice for you and your dog. This is general information that I think might be useful and helpful to experienced kayakers who wish to kayak with their dogs. All readers are advised to seek help from local competent professionals in the dog training and kayaking field before bringing a dog out on the water for the first time.

Step 1: INTRODUCING THE DOG TO WATER:

If the dog has not been taken swimming and has not been previously involved in water activities on a regular basis, the dog should first be introduced to these things. Some dogs initially do not seem to understand that dogs can't walk on water; they quite simply step into the water from the kayak, as if they're leaving your lap or starting down a set of stairs. While this might be a bit humorous to watch, it can be a traumatic experience for some dogs and it could hinder their progress.

As with training all new things, prior experiences are important; for example, dogs that have prior experience playing on, and jumping in from shore, docks, embankments, etc, might be less likely to try to walk on water when riding in a kayak for the first time. Associating prior fun activities with the new kayaking experience would be a tremendous help also. For example, if you and the dog frequent a swimming area that could also become a first launch area for kayaking, the dog would likely be more at ease and look at the experience as one more exciting adventure! Swimming with the life jacket on in non-emergency situations could help the dog feel more confident later if an emergency situation were to present itself. Let your creativity guide you, keeping in mind that the more steps you create in the learning process and the longer you take before moving onto the next step, the easier it will be for your dog.

STEP 2: INTRODUCING THE LIFE JACKET:

At this point you should have already purchased a life jacket and checked for proper fit. Review *"Will My Dog Need A Life Jacket"* in the prior question and answer section of this book if you have questions.

A BRIEF REVIEW:

Introduce your dog to its life jacket, if it is already familiar with water activities, but has not previously worn a life jacket. First, allow the dog to wear it during a few of its regular walks. Use this opportunity to re-check the fit of the jacket as the dog walks. If the jacket is hindering its ability to walk and/or pee freely, you will need to make adjustments or purchase a different jacket. Allow the dog to wear it into the water, checking to see if the dog can swim freely while the dog thinks it's all about free-swim time. Keep the dog close in case something goes wrong with the jacket during this test and introduction phase.

If the dog is comfortable and willing, gently tip the dog to one side and then release the dog, checking to be certain the jacket will right the dog and that its face is above water. Repeat on the other side. Please do not hold the dog on its side against its will or for a long length of time; you just want to quickly and very gently see if the jacket will right the dog without creating panic in the dog.

Please see "Will My Dog Need A Life Jacket" in the prior question and answer section of this book for more details. The more practice and prep, the better prepared you and your dog will be! And don't forget the fun!!!

Step 3: INTRODUCING THE KAYAK:

Put the kayak in which the dog will be riding on a section of lawn that is familiar to the dog and let the dog sniff and investigate all parts of the kayak. You could even leave the kayak in a place that the dog frequents for a few days, or longer, so that it sees it and gets to know its safe. Please don't reprimand or make a big deal of your dog marking territory on your kayak! It will wash off! Gently try to avoid it happening and gently discourage the dog from doing it again if it does happen; but, don't take all the fun out of this experience. Keep in mind a dog's perspective of fun and exploration is different from our own.

Step 4: GETTING TO KNOW THE KAYAK:

Sit in the kayak on a section of lawn that is familiar to the dog and invite the dog to join you. Let the dog decide when it's ready to enter the kayak. It's certainly ok to assist the dog if it's trying to get in; however, resist putting or pulling the dog inside before it has clearly indicated that it wants to be in the kayak with you. Allow the dog to get in and out, and back in again, as often as it will.

"OK, why are we staring at the horse and donkey?"

Randomly rewarding the dog with a small treat, say, every second, fifth, and sixth times… it enters the kayak would help encourage the dog to participate without creating the expectation that a treat should be given every time it enters the kayak. Randomly alternating treat delivery like this helps to avoid creating a solid pattern of reward and reduces the dog's continued expectation of a treat. After it's acclimated itself to the situation, you could start looking for opportunities to ask the dog to sit when it enters the kayak before getting a treat, starting to encourage the dog to enter and calm down.

Don't be too quick to take this next step or too adamant about the dog sitting and calming down at this point because this will come with time. You don't want to take the fun out of it; just attempt to *suggest and lead* your dog towards this wanted behavior whenever you see a *gentle opportunity* to do so. Again, prior training, involving the sit and quiet cues, would be helpful to this learning experience.

I'm not trying to humanize animals; however, our society in general doesn't give animals enough credit when it comes to their IQ. When introducing the dog to this and other situations, try to think about how you might introduce a very young child to such an experience. Most people would hopefully encourage a child to learn and progress while being patient with their limitations.

For example, they wouldn't likely demand that the child sit absolutely still right away unless it were a safety issue. Instead they would likely get the young child to sit still enough and then gently over time encourage them to understand that they need to sit still even more. I suggest being courteous and doing this with dogs as well, giving the dog the opportunity to reach its max potential! Over time, the kayaker will be rewarded with a dog that will start to think and learn more independently and outside specific lessons.

Try to end these sessions with the dog in the kayak with you. Reward the dog with a lot of praise and exit the kayak. Also try to end this exercise before the dog has become bored with it; you want to avoid extending it so long that the dog has become interested in other things. Short frequent sessions would be better than one long one!

Make sure that you do something fun with your dog after each of these practice sessions so that your dog associates leaving the kayak with doing something fun! For example, you don't want to end the session and then immediately give the dog the dreaded bath or take it to the vet for its annual vaccinations. On the other hand, you wouldn't want to end the sessions and then do something overly stimulating with the dog because then it may want to end these kayak practice sessions early to get to the more favored activity. This is part of the balancing act I spoke about earlier. Try not to view these sessions as training sessions, but as introductions to new things, while building on new experiences and growing over time. Teach, don't train!

Step 5: INTRODUCING EQUIPMENT:

Gradually introduce the necessary equipment that the dog will see and interact with while in the kayak. If the dog is obviously uneasy about an item, spend time reassuring the dog and getting it used to that specific item before you move on to the next one. Make sure the dog sees the paddle moving about you in various positions and your life jacket on and off of your body. Shake and freely move these items about. Tap the side of the kayak. "Bump" nearby items with your paddles so that the dog hears unusual noises. Rattle your feet around under the kayak deck. If the dog gets used to more movement and noise than it will witness on the water in the kayak, it should do better with the initial trip when there is less movement and noise.

If you secure an item like indoor/outdoor carpeting to the deck of your kayak so that the dog can stand without slipping, you should introduce the dog to this aspect at this time as well. *See Chapter 4 for more details about the deck mat.*

During this time, you could also invite your dog to sit in the kayak on the lawn and rock it slightly to show the dog that the boat doesn't always stay absolutely still. Don't rush the process and do this during the initial introductions to the kayak; small progressive steps are far better than rushing the process! We don't want our dogs tolerating new items and situations! We want them to learn to trust and accept them and that takes time.

Step 6: CHOOSING A SITE:

This is an example of a nice boat ramp for a dog's first time out on the water.

Choose a fellow paddler/friend, and invite them to come with you and aid you in selecting a site. This person could also provide assistance and support during your dog's first trip out on the water and take lots of photos!

Choose a kayaking site that would be good for beginning kayakers. First, visit the site without your dog so that you are not distracted by the dog and you can better take in the full situation. Read posted rules and regulations. If dogs are not allowed, please honor this regulation and choose a different site.

During this initial site visit, envision what you think is going to happen. Consider things like, how easy it will be for you to get in and out of the water. You don't want a situation where you'll be rocking the kayak around. Try to find a situation where you can easily glide away from the launch area and return in that same easy fashion. Does it look like you will have easy paddling or does it look like you might get hung up in weeds and lily pads? You want a site with easy clear paddling; a smooth uneventful first experience. Picking a smaller lake or pond that doesn't permit speed boats and jet skis is best. Do some creative thinking and ask for input from your friend or others who are familiar with the sites you are considering.

Don't over look not using the ramp at all. I have, in some cases, looked at boat ramps and thought, what were they thinking, and used a nice grassy area near the ramp to enter and exit. Also consider things like will you be able to park close to the ramp where it would be more convenient for a person with a dog or will you have to unload at the launch and then park far away and walk your dog along a busy road or large parking area to get back to the ramp. Keeping in mind that having a calm unstressed dog entering the kayak is best.

Try out the site without your dog. Paddle around the pond or lake with your friend/fellow paddler and evaluate its positive aspects and also its short-comings. Discuss these as you paddle about. If after being out on the water, you think its not a good location, do more research and visit another site, repeating the process.

Even if you don't live in the Connecticut area, consider viewing the sites that I have marked as possible beginner sites on my website to see what they have in common with potential sites in your area: KayakingCTwithLou.com *(Category: Life Saver)*

STEP 7: THE RIGHT DAY

Next, I suggest that you visit the site with your dog, but without kayaking, and then again on a different day when you'll take your dog out on the water with you for the first time *(more details in the next two sections below)*. Choose a nice day that is not windy and is of a comfortable temperature and humidity for both your dog's first non-kayaking visit to the site and for its first trip on the water! You don't want a scorching hot day or a freezing cold day for the dog's first site visit and its first kayaking experiences. Weekdays will generally be less busy than Saturday or Sunday; Weekday mornings and early afternoonsare less busy than after the average workday ends.

Also be sure to pick days when you're not feeling rushed; ones where you can take all day if needed to step back in the process and review a previous step or create a training experience for an unexpected situation. You want to be relaxed and not thinking about other things; leave worry and concerns behind and be in the moment with your dog and its new kayaking experience. If you're not at some points laughing and smiling, you're not getting what this is all about; relax and have fun! Bring your camera and take lots of photos.

Tiny on deck and caught in the rain on Ashland Pond in Jewett City, Connecticut, USA.

STEP 8: INITIAL SITE VISIT WITH YOUR DOG

Take your dog to the site for a non-kayaking visit. Play ball or Frisbee if its safe to do so or take a walk along the shore, allowing the dog to test and play in the water if safe to do so. You might want to stick to a walk if you have an overly excitable dog because you don't want it getting hyped up to play Frisbee the next time you come to this area with your kayak and end up with a dog that can't calm down. If your dog is generally calm and not easily over excited, playing Frisbee or ball should be an acceptable activity at the new site if it's safe to do so. If it's not safe for the dog to be walked along the shore in the area of the boat launch, its probably not a safe place for a dog's first experience in a kayak either.

Many people skip steps like these, not realizing how important they really are. Envision for a moment that a friend is going to take you up in a hot-air balloon for the first time and you're very nervous about it.

Scenario 1: Without saying where or what you'll be doing, your friend takes you to a location where you'll be going up in a hot air balloon five minutes before the balloon will be launched. Your friend explains that they have pre-paid so you feel obligated to try it even though you're very nervous and caught off guard. How do you feel?

Scenario 2: Now imagine that your friend takes you to the event location the day before the event and you get to see balloons being launched and your friend explains the process to you.

Which experience is the one that would make you feel most comfortable about this new activity? We can't explain the kayaking process to the dog; but, we can help them understand that the launch site is a safe friendly place before bringing them there for their first kayaking trip!

OPTIONAL: I might pack up all my kayaking equipment before making this initial trip so that the dog associates the equipment and kayak being loaded with going to this destination. You and your dog could also wear your life jackets at the location if you've done the steps previously presented in this book. Your friend could also unload the kayak and leave it unused by the boat launch while you play with and/or walk the dog if it's safe and appropriate to do so. Let the dog sniff and investigate the kayak in the new location. You could get in and invite the dog to get in and out of the kayak IF the dog is willing and wants to do this; resist pulling or putting the dog into the kayak until it is clearly asking to get in. All these things could better prepare your dog for its first trip; whether you do them or not should be determined by the level of your dog's comfort/acceptance and safety issues related to that particular site and the equipment being used.

Step 9: BEFORE THE FIRST RIDE

Being in a kayak and on the water is a new experience for a dog. For example, my dog didn't understand that he couldn't just simply step off the deck of the kayak and onto lily pads until he fell in a few times. I tried to save him from these learning experiences by telling him "no" each time he tried, but he would eventually try it when my attention was drawn to other things and he would fall in. I would literally snap a photo and hear a splash!

Remarkably, once he learned that he couldn't walk on lily pads, he also had to learn he couldn't step out onto similar but different plants that covered the water. He didn't make the connection that all plants and algae growing on water are unstable; he had to learn this individually.

This new experience will also require that you make minor, but important, adjustments to how you paddle. For example, you don't want to be doing any of those fancy tight quick turns or your dog will be in the drink! You will also need to compensate for the dog similar to carrying a passenger on a motorcycle. For example, if the dog leans or stands to one side or the other, the kayak might start to drift if you don't compensate for the imbalance. Initially, you will have to concentrate on remembering to do these things, but after a while they will become automatic.

I always have my paddle secured to the kayak with a piece of coated rope because I often kayak alone. I would suggest that you consider doing this when kayaking with your dog. If you have to reach for your dog or do something related to your dog and you drop your paddles in the water, you can more easily retrieve it if it's secured to the kayak and not floating away out of reach!

You can purchase a line specifically made for this or use a piece of coated rope as I do. If you do this, make sure it's not too long: you don't want it long enough to get wrapped around you or your dog's neck if the boat is tipped over; but, long enough that you can comfortably use the paddles! If you've never used this type of set-up before, I advise you to seek help from a local kayaking professional before doing it.

You also may not want to choose this option if you think it might be too much for you to handle with the leash also being involved--I'm tossing it out there so you're aware of the option, but you must decide if you think it is a safe option for you and your dog and act accordingly.

A mat or rubber backed rug on the bottom of the kayak that extends from the seat in the cockpit area into the area under the deck would be appreciated by just about every dog. Make sure the back is grippy and test it to be sure it won't slip when you step in and out of the kayak! Even if it doesn't initially slip, be cautious when getting in and out because it might become slippery when it gets wet or dirty. I have a mat in the kayak every time I go out with my dog because he sometimes sits in the cockpit area and its nicer for him to sit on that rather than sitting directly on the cold hard bottom of my kayak..

I've seen dogs new to kayaking go under the deck of the kayak for a few minutes and then reappear more willing to engage in the environment after they realize the boat isn't going to sink, so I would encourage you to consider doing this at least for your dog's first trip. I use two pieces of carpet/mat with rubber backs that I bought for $1 each at the Dollar Store. My dog also has gone under the deck of my kayak for short periods of time on a couple of occasions when a cloudy day unexpectedly became a very sunny and hot day with very little shade where we were paddling.

Tiny checking out some geese on the river in Voluntown, Connecticut, USA.

Choose a calm friendly paddling friend to assist you with your dog's first ride; someone not easily frazzled and who can help and also give moral support if needed--and take photos! Animals look to the people around them for reassurance. If you or your helper is nervous, uptight, or feeling rushed, this won't help your dog feel safe and calm. You also don't want a friend/helper who tends to be a perfectionist! One of your laid back go-with-the-flow friends would be better as long as they are a competent kayaker. Be very particular about who you ask to help with this initial experience. If the person is willing, you could also bring them along on the initial non-kayaking visits to the site.

Step 10: THE FIRST RIDE

Don't fish or introduce and inter-mingle other activities at this time. Focus on your dog and making this trip fun and safe for everyone. Ask your friend to unload the kayaks and equipment while you give your dog time to acclimate itself to the location. Take the dog for a walk around the area and down to the water. If you've done the previous steps, your dog should be familiar with the site. This will also give your dog the opportunity to relieve itself before it gets into the kayak.

When you feel that the dog is calm and understanding of the situation, put on its and your life jackets and repeat steps 4 & 5 at the boat launch or in close proximity to the launch. Then rock the kayak a little to inform the dog that in this new location it might move differently than it did on your lawn.

If you first do this near the launch, repeat the process with the kayak in the water at the launch area if it is safe to do so. If it's not safe to do so, I recommend you stop and pick a different launch area.

It's very important that you don't rush the dog. Let the dog get into the kayak on its own when it's ready. It's certainly ok to assist the dog if it's trying to get in, but resist any temptation to put it inside before it's asking to get in! If you let the dog make the choice to get in, you'll avoid rushing the dog into a situation that its not ready to experience.

STEP 11: THE LAUNCH

With you, your dog, and all your necessary gear in the kayak, have your friend gently push your kayak off from the launch. Having someone do this for you will make the transition smoother for the dog and it will free your hands so that you can get underway and assist your dog if need be. When you return to the ramp, have your friend exit first and help you smoothly get ashore with your dog.

I would recommend that you not let the dog stand on the deck for the initial launch experience; keep it inside with you and let it choose whether it wants to get up on the deck after you're out on the water and settled. Initially stay close to the launch area in case the dog panics or has some other need to go ashore.

When/if your dog decides to go up on the deck of the kayak, you will have to adjust your paddling to accommodate your dog. Do everything slower so that the dog has time to figure what it needs to do in order to balance itself in this new environment. You'll need to make conscious adjustments to your balance as well; you'll get used to doing this and it will, in time, become an unconscious act.

For example, if my dog is laying to one side of the kayak or standing with his weight more to one side, the kayak will start to drift similar to if I were sitting hunched incorrectly to one side. I adjust my body slightly and/or paddle lighter on one side than the other when the dog creates this slight imbalance. Like I mentioned earlier, at first this will require your attention; but after a while, you'll do it without thinking about it.

Allow the dog to sit where ever it feels most comfortable as long as it is safe to do so. This allows the dog to acclimate itself to the new environment.

Offer a lot of praise when the dog is trying and behaving in a manner that is acceptable to you! When giving reassurance, be certain you're not coddling the dog or creating concern in the dog by making too much fuss over the dog's moments of concern or hesitation. Let the dog own the experience; for example, don't try to over manipulate the situation by repositioning the dog on the deck every time it slips or stumbles. Try to resist giving too much attention to poor balance, etc., and be encouraging of the dog's accomplishments. If the dog goes up on the deck and wobbles about, let it figure out how it needs to stand. It's ok to stop or slow down to help ease the pressure, but resist the desire to reach out and reposition the dog unless it's about to fall.

It's ok to go a very short distance and float while the dog tries out the new environment, and then return to shore! Don't feel like you have to be paddling because you're in a kayak! Keep in mind that it will sometimes take the dog more than a few trips to get the hang of it.

Don't set yourself up for failure by trying to make everything perfect! The experience won't be perfect; but, your dog is not expecting perfection and will be very forgiving of mistakes. Keep this first trip very short. It's best that the experience end on a happy note and not with the dog begging to get out. So don't wait too long to end the first trip! Small gradual steps work best when teaching animals!

SHOULD I?

I have helped many people with training issues, especially those with horses. I often get questions that start with "should I do this or that?" I'm not talking about should I use a harness or collar. I mean real hefty issues like "should I ride my horse that pushes and rubs me on the fence; but, is otherwise a real sweetie..." or something along the lines of "should I go out in my kayak with my dog if I have only paddled 2 times; I'm not 'new' to kayaking if I've been out 2 times, right?" By the very fact that a person asks a training related question starting with "should I (proceed to do....)" tells me that they don't believe that they are ready to do what they're asking about!

The person asking may not realize that they already know the answer to this question; but to me, it is very obvious that they are not ready to take that next step. A person's level of experience and their dog's level of training, should be such that the person feels very confident in taking the dog out on the water for the first time otherwise they shouldn't do it!

Sooooo, if you feel yourself wanting to ask "should I (proceed to do....)" stop and re-evaluate why you're asking the question and fix whatever it is that is causing your self doubt. It may be a confidence issue or it may be something of more significance. If after you re-evaluate and revisit the training process, you still feel the need to ask, then contact a competent and well-seasoned dog trainer and/or a competent professional kayak instructor in your area and ask for help!

A young pup (left) waiting to take to the water in a canoe at Billings Lake.

7 PROBLEM SOLVING

Tiny on deck enjoying some late afternoon sunshine in Canterbury, Connecticut, USA.

PROBLEMS: THE WHINER

I want to be clear that I'm going to be discussing dogs that whine and **NOT** dogs that are in a state of panic, and/or overwhelmed, and I'm assuming that dog owners should, and would, know the difference. If you're not absolutely sure of this difference, please seek help from a professional dog trainer before continuing.

The number one concern I've heard from paddlers is that some dogs whine while kayaking and some people suggest that these dogs should not be taken along on paddling trips. I disagree! I don't believe a dog should be excluded from kayaking trips simply because the dog whines without first trying to help the dog overcome this unwanted behavior.

It's important to understand that when a dog whines, it's trying to tell us something. For example, wouldn't we feel a bit foolish if we were complaining about a whining dog, when finally it squeezes its hind legs together, taking on that shaky half squat that causes us to think it needs to pee! Ooops!

If you can determine a trigger for the behavior, such as the dog only whines when....then you have a dog with a trigger. If you have a dog that seems to constantly whine no matter what is or isn't changing around it, you have a dog without an apparent trigger; doesn't mean there isn't one, it just means the whining is more generalized and does not seem to be related to something specific. I will discuss whining with a trigger first, and then the more general type of whining in the next section.

Tiny chillin' with Cec on Aspinook Pond in Griswold, Connecticut, USA.

THE WHINER WITH A TRIGGER:

I want to be clear that I'm going to be discussing dogs that whine and NOT dogs that are in a state of panic, aggressive, and/or overwhelmed, and I'm assuming that dog owners should, and would, know the difference. If you're new to dog ownership, not an adult, and/or otherwise not absolutely sure of this difference, please seek help from a professional dog trainer before continuing.

I'm now going to discuss two different ways I would approach whiners with a trigger:

1. What a dog wants….

The first approach involves identifying the trigger and then only rewarding the dog with what it wants when it's behaving in a manner that is acceptable to the kayaker. For example, suppose the dog gets excited whenever it sees the boat ramp and starts to whine and wiggle around, making it difficult to paddle and line up properly with the ramp. In this case, the sight of the boat ramp and/or the expectation of what will happen after arriving at the boat ramp is the dog's trigger.

In either case, I would turn the kayak away from the ramp whenever the dog started to whine and wiggle around, and only start back towards the ramp when the dog had stopped, reassuring it with a "good boy/girl" whenever I turned back towards the ramp and it was behaving as I wanted. As soon as it started acting up again, I would turn away and paddle in the opposite direction, only turning back towards the ramp when the dog was behaving appropriately again.

In this case, the reward for not whining is going towards what the dog wants which is the boat ramp; what the dog wants (going towards the ramp) is taken away when the dog is whining. The dog is rewarded with what it wants only when it's not whining. Some dogs will get this right away, especially those that have been trained using this method in other situations. Other dogs might take more time to catch on to what is going on; but, this is a powerful tool if you have the patience to take it to the end point.

It's very important to remain consistent, even if that means only paddling two strokes before changing direction again. You might reach a point where you literally adjust your paddles as if going to turn and the dog stops whining. If this happens you can continue without fully turning away if the dog remains quiet and still.

This could be practiced a few times whenever paddling in the area of the boat launch as well as during future trips. Each time, it should take less effort and time if the sessions are reasonably close together and the person is consistent.

It shouldn't be expected that the dog will remember this the next time out; I would do this a few times before I would expect to see it becoming part of the dog's behavior pattern. I would also expect the dog to test me on a few occasions just to be sure that I actually mean it and plan to stick with it.

If a person only paddled with their dog once a year, it would be unfair to expect the dog to do well. The more this method is used with the dog, the more quickly it would understand the process, and the more quickly the person would start to see a positive change in the overall situation. If a paddler is using this method for the first time, it will take longer than the second and third situation in which it's used. The most efficient use of this method would be to use it on land and on water.

I would at the same time try to consider why the dog is so excited to see the boat ramp. For example, has the dog missed its meal time being out on the water? Could adjustments be made to the timing of the next trip, or could the dog's meal be brought along, so that it doesn't have to skip meal time and be overly eager to get home? Was the kayaking trip longer than was comfortable for the dog? Is there an activity that occurs immediately after arriving at the launch that is of more value to the dog than kayaking? These are only a few things to get you thinking about what might be going on. Use your knowledge of your dog and the specific situation to brain storm reasons and possible solutions for your specific situation.

Whenever an animal is presenting unwanted behaviors, implement a training solution; but, also ALWAYS try to figure out why the behavior is happening! The real and long-term solutions are in knowing why it's occurring in the first place!

2. Bust that myth…

Before I discuss this next training method, I would like to dispel a myth that I hear far to often; many people wrongly believe that food reward training means that dog owners will have to continue to give the animal food rewards long after training is complete, when in fact the opposite is true. When done correctly, more food rewards are given in the beginning, and then less and less are given over time until NO food reward is given for the learned behavior!

That's right, NONE! The end result of food reward training (done correctly) is NO food given for the learned behavior! So often we see people teaching and rewarding an animal for doing a trick and this causes many people to think that is food reward or clicker training in its entirety; but, it's not.

"What the heck was that!?!?"

Beyond Theory: *Food Reward Training*

Even if you're adamantly against this training method, please read this entire section and give it fair consideration because what many people think is food reward training is not even close.

I want to say right up front that I don't believe clicker and food reward training should be considered stand-alone methods of training. I use them often; however, I view them as tools/methods to be utilized within other training methods. I personally blend many training methods together.

I used food reward training with our dog Tiny while kayaking because he initially whined whenever he saw a dog or person on shore. The complete process which I used is not intro-level training; however, I'm going to explain this process in an attempt to dispel the evil myths surrounding food reward training and so that you can better understand the process if a trainer suggests doing it with your dog.

This is not intended to replace instruction from a professional dog trainer. The following section is an overview of how I used food reward training to teach my dog to stop whining in a particular situation; it is not a training guide. I hope that this section will encourage you to hire a trainer to teach you how to do this complete method and that this section will supplement that training.

My dog whined and occasionally let out a bark whenever he saw a person or dog on shore. So, I started the training process by making an effort to pay close attention to what was going on along the shoreline and specifically tried to locate people and dogs before my dog saw them.

I did this because training an animal to stop an unwanted behavior is usually easiest if the training is implemented before the animal becomes engaged in the unwanted behavior. If I waited until the animal was doing the behavior, I would be re-active and I want to be pro-active when training animals. A person who is being re-active is not in control of the situation because they are reacting to what is going on around them and playing catch-up; they are not controlling what is going on around them. A common reactive behavior would be to yell at the dog or be over-bearing and domineering with the dog whenever the dog was whining and/or barking.

I've also seen people behave in a reactive manner and attempt to use food to stop an animal from doing an unwanted behavior while the animal is engaged in doing the "bad" behavior. This is detrimental at so many levels. From a perspective of food reward training, it is reinforcing the bad behavior and encouraging the animal to do the unwanted behavior more! The person is likely thinking that if they give the treat the dog will stop whining. Well, the dog doesn't understand these intentions; it only understands that--ok, I was whining and they gave me kibbles while I was whining, so I guess, I should whine more to get more kibbles. Whatever the dog is doing when it gets the treat/reward is the behavior that the dog is being asked to do more! If you feel like you're bribing the animal to behave, re-access what you're doing.

If I saw the person/dog before Tiny saw them and before he started to whine, I would remove a treat from the treat bag and say good boy and give him the treat. At this point, I was rewarding him for being quiet before he saw the trigger and before he thought about whining. I was being pro-active and taking charge of the situation by setting an expectation of behavior before he saw the trigger. *I marked the good behavior that I wanted to continue.*

I continued to give him treats at set intervals as we passed the person or dog on shore. I based the timing of the treat delivery on my experience training animals. For example, if I thought he seemed more focused on the trigger, I would deliver the treats more often. If he were more focused on me and the treats than on the trigger, I would give treats less frequently as I continued by the trigger.

Someone new to this type of training might benefit from counting between each treat delivery and not worry so much about giving more or less. It's better to give too many than too few treats at this point. For example, I might give a treat and count 1, 2 and give another treat, count 1,2 and give another treat, and maybe even repeat this sequence one more time before paddling; this would help solidify a pattern of expectation in the dog before continuing to paddle by the trigger. Then I might count 1 set of paddle strokes and give a treat, 1 set of paddle strokes and give a treat, continuing to repeat this pattern until the kayak is past the trigger and the dog's focus is away from the trigger and on something new.

If the dog seems fine with that, I might start counting 2 sets of paddle strokes between treats for the next series of treats, continuing to increase or decrease time between treats based on the dog's behavior. Counting gives a person who is new to this method a way to gauge if they are giving more or less treats and if they are progressing within the method. If your trainer suggests this method and you're new to doing this type of training, I suggest you use this counting method.

Whenever my dog saw a person or dog before I did, and he started whining, I ignored him and paddled past the person/dog. If he started whining while getting treats for not whining, I simply stopped giving treats, put the treat bag out of sight, and ignored him. This requires more than pretending to ignore the animal. The paddler can't just pretend to ignore the animal; they must truly and completely ignore it. The dog owner can't be fuming about the dog whining and be ignoring it. They can't be thinking I'm never going to get him to stop and be genuinely ignoring it.

Envision yourself at home in your living room. Your dog is whining so you pick up a newspaper or book, kick back in the recliner, put the open book or paper up in front of your face, and read; that is convincing. A paddler in the above situation needs to be as convincing in the kayak.

I've seen trainers tell people look away or look down. These trainers don't take into consideration an animal's keen intuitive nature; they are only considering their own IQ and what they perceive to be the dog's lack of any significant IQ. It is true that animals don't have the same IQ as a person; however, they have more intuition than any human is going to muster! The dog must believe that you're not just pretending, and that you really don't care that they are whining, and that there is no chance in… that they will benefit from whining. It will usually take more than one time for a whining dog to be convinced. Believe it and feel it and they will come to believe it too!

It might be helpful to accept the whining for what it is; while it might create a few moments of annoyance for you and the person or dog on shore, in the grand scheme of things, it's an infrequent and minute problem to be trying to overcome. Don't make an issue like this into something bigger than what it is…take a deep breath and relax. Don't worry about what people might think about your dog whining; in a few minutes, they will have moved on to thinking about something else.

I also praised my dog whenever he stopped whining, even if that was minutes later! This is another mistake made by many people that are new to training; it's unfair to only correct or ignore the animal when it is doing something "wrong" without also being clear about what behavior we do want in that situation!

If a dog owner ignores or reprimands an animal for an unwanted behavior, they should also tell the pet good boy/girl as soon it has stopped doing the unwanted behavior so that it knows what behavior is acceptable for that situation! Imagine the state of confusion and anxiety you would experience if you were repeatedly told you were wrong; but, not told when you were right!

Suppose I said to you, "That's not right, move a little to your left…more…more…" And that was all I said. I didn't clarify if I wanted you to stop or continue to move after that last request. Wouldn't you feel better if I clarified what I wanted by saying something like, "OK. *(That's where I want you to stand.)*"

The same happens with animals when people say or imply that the animal should stop doing an unwanted behavior; but, aren't clear about what the animal should be doing. If the dog owner ignores a bad behavior or corrects a bad behavior, they should ALWAYS praise the animal for returning to a wanted behavior after misbehaving. This will help to reduce anxiety in the animal and they will have more respect for the person.

I repeated this process every time I saw a person or dog on shore before my dog saw them. I sometimes came back by the same person/dog later in the same paddling session to reinforce the behavior, being careful to not over do it or do it again too soon.

Tiny on deck on Ross Pond in Danielson, Connecticut, USA.

After a few trips out on the water and several training opportunities, I started to see my dog becoming more relaxed as we passed the triggers. As the dog became more relaxed, I gave less and less treats as we passed the triggers. This is an important aspect of the training process that is often over looked.

Gauging progress at this point requires evaluating the dogs level of relaxation because this method does not actually teach the animal to not whine and bark; it teaches the dog to relax down to a level where it doesn't feel the need to whine in the presence of the trigger. It's important to realize this distinction. If I had chosen a method of training that taught the dog to not whine and bark, then the dog would also likely not whine or bark when it saw a perceived threat! This method that I chose leaves that opportunity on the table because I'm changing the whining/barking threshold; I'm not saying don't whine or bark!

Keep in mind that the dog will relax faster if the paddler is relaxed! Don't rush this process and don't let it consume you. It's just something to work on with no set time for it's completion! And it will of course depend greatly on how many times the trigger is encountered.

I eventually reached a point where I had decreased the number of treats being given to a point where my dog was only receiving one treat for passing the trigger. At this point, when I passed the trigger, I started what is called chaining behaviors. Instead of giving the treat for having successfully passed the person/dog without whining, I immediately asked my dog to do a previously learned trick--I asked him to bow. Any previously learned trick that is safely done in/on a kayak can be used. Tiny just happens to like to bow.

Bowing has now been successfully added to the behavior chain. The sequence now went as follows: identify the trigger before the dog, compliment the dog to mark the good behavior, paddle past the trigger, immediately ask the dog to bow, and give the treat for bowing. He was at this point receiving a treat for bowing and no longer receiving a treat for passing the trigger. I know what some of you are thinking! You're thinking, so what, it's still getting a treat for bowing! Patience...

At this point, I started to phase out the treat. I would sometimes pass the trigger, request a bow, and then treat for the bow. Other times I would pass the trigger and make a huge fuss, saying something like, Oh, aren't you such a good boy," and invite him into my lap and scratch behind his ears and rub his belly…

In the beginning of this phase out process, I would ask for, and treat, the bow more often. As I saw the dog relaxing and being more and more accepting of receiving praise vs. treat, I would ask for the bow less and less often until it was no longer necessary to do it. The final phase of this training would be to praise the dog with less and less enthusiasm for passing the trigger and offer the praise randomly and less often.

I can do this phase out portion of the training very quickly because I've done it with animals so much that I don't even think about doing it; it unfolds and happens. Someone new to this training method might struggle with it a little, and that's ok, because it's a very flexible and forgiving process.

In doing this process in this way, I took an issue of whining and gradually deflated it, transforming it into a gradually smaller and easier issue to deal with. Eliminating one treat and moments of praise are far easier to accomplish than the bigger issue of a whining dog! It's like gradually deflating a balloon vs. popping it. The dog learned over time to be calmer and calmer around the trigger until it reached a point where it no longer felt a need to whine.

Sure the dog could've probably been reprimanded and even bullied into not whining; but, at what cost? This behavior change in my dog was accomplished without either of us feeling bad about the training method or the results. If anything, it strengthened the bond between us.

I advise against any method of dealing with this situation that might create an absolute because you might, at some point, want the dog to warn you of a perceived threat. Using the method I described, changes the threshold of whining and barking; the dog would still most likely inform you of a perceived threat because the threat would be of a higher stimulation and the dog was never told to not bark or whine.

Please don't be over-bearing and domineering with the dog and demand that it stop barking and stay quiet and do this over and over again. By doing this, you would not be setting a threshold boundary as in the method I described; you would be telling the dog this is unwanted behavior-- period. It is reactive behavior, not pro-active, and it has the negative effects that I previously mentioned. A dog experiencing this type of *training* may or may not warn you of a perceived threat depending on how over-bearing and persistent the person was in the initial situations. Be very careful before creating an absolute; make sure you're never going to want that behavior for some other reason!

I caution you to not simply distract your dog every time you pass a trigger to keep the dog from whining. For example, you see the trigger and fuss over your dog until you're past the trigger. Doing this might work once or twice to *avoid* the issue, but it's not likely to provide enough long-term incentive to fix the problem like receiving treats will. It's more like avoiding the issue and hoping it goes away than addressing it and it can, in some cases, create more problems.

These are the reasons why I suggest the food reward training process; it actually addresses the problem, and done correctly, should help stop the escalation of this type of problem and stop that annoying whining behavior from creeping into other areas. While at the same time, not discouraging the dog from informing you of someone or something that it perceives to be a threat. This is the method that I have found works most often and it's a very dog friendly approach.

This method can also be practiced at a dog park because a dog that does this in the kayak will likely do the same or similar at the dog park. Have the whiner stand or sit and behave quietly as dogs and people approach and pass by it on the walking trails etc using this same technique. It should be quite helpful to do this at the dog park because approaching people/dogs are likely to be encountered more often at the dog park than the dog is likely to pass people and dogs in a kayak. And a dog that whines at people and dogs from in a kayak probably does it to some degree elsewhere.

This was an example of chaining behaviors and phasing out rewards. An alternate phase out method would be to build on the behavior. When chaining behaviors in the above example, I added the bow which was unrelated to the outcome. Building on a behavior would mean that I add something to a behavior that will remain as part of the learned behavior chain.

An example of building on a behavior might go like this: Say, I taught a dog to sit using food reward training and now I don't want to give a treat for sitting; so I build on the behavior. The initial training sequence is that I ask the dog to sit and reward it with a treat. At this point, I'm going to add a behavior to that sequence. The sequence might now go as follows: Request the dog sit and the dog sits; but instead of rewarding that, I then ask the dog to focus on my face and not the treat before receiving the reward. So the behavior chain is now as follows; sit, focus, treat. I built on the requested behavior by adding something that I will always want to happen when the dog is asked to sit. *(Teaching an animal to focus on you and not the food/treat is very beneficial.)*

Once the dog has learned to sit and focus on my face and not the food, I could then start working on teaching the dog to "stay." So now I would have the dog sit, look at me, and stay before getting a treat. Do you see how I'm now building on the behavior and that I'm no longer treating the dog for the initial "sit" behavior?

Once I got to this point, I would teach the dog to stay longer and longer and until I was out of sight and returned. This is the point where I would wean them from a treat. For example, when I went out of sight and returned, I would reward them for this only until it was a solid behavior pattern. Then I might start returning and becoming very animated and excited like when I come home from work; the dog will usually forget about the treat and reciprocate with excitement about my return. While the dog is still excited to see me, but after I've acknowledged it, I would quickly move the dog onto doing something else before it has time to think, "*hey, I didn't get a treat.*" I would alternate this with receiving a treat for returning into their sight and phase out the treat as I did in the previous example. This method doesn't require a previously taught trick as was the case in the first example of the dog whining at people and dogs.

When working with this training method for as long as I have, the handler will more quickly recognize when to build on a behavior or start to wean the rewards using a previously trained trick. Until that time, follow your trainers instruction, have fun with it, and learn and grow with your pet and your understanding of the process.

I'm going to give you another example of the technique being used; but this time, I will combine building on the behavior with using the always rewarded trick. I'm going to use a very different example using a horse so that you might see it from a new perspective.

Suppose I used food reward training to teach my horse to accept a halter and I want to now be able to halter my horse without giving a treat for it. I would put on the halter and give the usual treat until there was a solid pattern of consistent behavior; then, the next time I put on the halter, I would immediately point to his barrel (the always rewarded trick) and say get your barrel instead of rewarding him for accepting the halter. In doing this I have added the barrel trick to the behavior chain. Instead of putting on the halter and giving a treat, I am now putting on the halter, having the horse do the trick, and then treating the horse for doing the trick.

The horse's enthusiasm for doing the barrel trick and always getting a reward for it redirects his attention away from thinking about not getting a reward for the halter being put on. I sometimes see a split second moment of confusion, but the animal's focus will go to the request for the always rewarded trick if the trick has been reinforced enough! Over the next several times that the halter is put on I would randomly alternate giving a treat, asking him to do the barrel trick, and still other times build on the behavior by asking the horse to do something else like lower its head or quickly walk him over to another activity.

Over time I would increase the number of times that I walked with him to another activity or built on the behavior and decreased the number of times I asked for the barrel trick, always being sure to be random and not form any patterns. This part of the process usually works very quickly to eliminate a food reward being given for haltering the horse. It is best to have a "trick" that is always rewarded and done often enough that the animal expects a treat for it every time.

If I haven't alternated my requests enough or I've progressed too quickly, the animal might do the trick without being asked to do it. If the animal does the trick without being asked for the behavior, I simply chuckle and ask for him to do it again, treat him, and move on. Asking him to re-do the trick or do a different trick puts me back in the leader role without disappointing the animal. I'm not rewarding them for doing it when they thought it was time to do it, I'm rewarding them for doing it when I asked for the behavior to be done again.

This is an indication that I need to back up a step in the process or that I need to be more random in my requests. I find this situation to be very exciting because the animal is thinking beyond what it's being told to do! It's anticipating. I never want to trash that process by thinking oh I didn't ask for this behavior so the animal doesn't deserve a treat. Instead, I re-engage the animal and ask it to repeat that trick or do a different trick and treat when the animal does it! No harm done and everyone is happy!

This is advanced training and a lot to toss at you at one time. I'm only presenting this partial summation because I want to dispel the myths that loom incorrectly around this method and encourage you to find a local trainer and learn this method; to do that, I had to give you an introduction to it so that you could better understand the process. As you can see from this section, there is a lot more to food reward and clicker training than most people realize. There is more to it than was presented here!

Tiny looking out over the falls at Wacky Pond in Sterling, Connecticut, USA

To click or not to click…

Sometimes people that are new to this training method do better using a training clicker that can be purchased for a few dollars online or at local pet stores. A clicker has a real benefit to the beginner because the clicker can identify a split second of time where saying something like good boy or girl cannot.

For example, if a dog were whining and something caught its attention just long enough that the dog gave it a glance and stopped whining, I could click the clicker to mark the behavior (the silence) and treat, letting it know that few seconds of silence was why it's being rewarded. In this case, once I marked the behavior, I could quickly start the process that I presented earlier in this chapter. This would be a variation of that method. There is a lot to learn within this training method; it is so much more than what most people think it is.

Saying good boy or girl takes longer to say than a click --and saying the words might overlap the dog beginning to whine again. So for this reason, I would suggest getting a clicker if you intend to advance within this training method.

I have seen people make a clucking noise to replace the sound of a clicker and I've tried doing this myself. I found that its doable; however, the verbal noise is not as loud and crisp as a clicker. I also found it to be quite annoying. The couple of dollars that it costs to buy a clicker, I recommend buying the clicker.

I've taught some useful and some really silly things using a clicker. For example, I taught my horse the cue "ears." If you're not familiar with horses, they flick their ears independently depending on what is attracting their attention. So when taking a photo, a horse's ears could be moving all over the place. If I say "ears," my horse will perk up with both ears solidly forward for the photo. LOL! This was taught using this method.

I sometimes use a clicker and other times not, depending on what it is that I'm teaching. For example, I taught my horse to blow through a noise tube. LOL Teaching this made it necessary to pick out exact moments of time when he was moving towards the wanted behaviors. For example, with the noise tube, I had to identify the moments when the horse exhaled air out his nostrils and I had to then encourage him to breathe heavier and harder through the tube so that it would make the noise. The click & treats would tell this well-seasoned trick trained horse when he was moving in the right direction. In most other situations where I don't need to capture a split-second of time, like an exhale of air, I just say "good" or "good boy."

And say it with enthusiasm! Animals better recognize when a person is happy about something if they show it with enthusiasm. I even jump up and down and clap sometimes. In positive environments, dogs and horses are such people-pleasers!

I've found that this type of training works faster for owners and animals that are familiar with this training method. I find that a dog trained to do other things using this method will most likely get this faster than a dog and owner who are new to food reward training. That just means that teaching your dog something using this method would make the next teaching moment easier!

If you're reading this and you don't have an issue like whining to address, consider having a local trainer show you how to teach some tricks to your dog using this method. If you do this, the method will be familiar to your dog when you find yourself in a situation where you want to use it and it's a lot of fun.

Trick training is also fun and stimulating for animals. Consider yourself coming home from work every day and doing the same routine day after day; then one day someone invites you to learn scuba diving! You feel recharged by the new experience and the break in your boring routine. In the same way, teaching tricks to animals stimulates their brains and breaks their ho-hum routine. It also gives the animal the knowledge that they can do the trick with a guarantee that both you and your dog will be satisfied and happy with this behavior! What a confidence builder!

You can't be perfect so don't beat yourself up over what might seem to be little set backs or mistakes. You're learning and your dog is learning and you're both progressing. Be proud of your accomplishments no matter how small, or how long it takes, because you'll get faster and better with more practice. Improvements are always a good thing even if we're not progressing as fast as we would like! And mistakes are just opportunities to learn!

NOTE: The food reward being given must be something of real interest to the dog, but it's better if it isn't of very high value to the dog. This is part of the balancing act I referred to earlier. Don't use it's favorite treat so that it becomes overly focused on the treats and not the lesson. Conversely, don't give a treat that is of so little significance that the dog isn't interested in participating for the treats. You want a treat somewhere in the middle. I don't give big pieces of treat either; if I'm using a big treat, I'll break it up into smaller pieces slightly bigger than a food kibble and in some cases I use food kibbles.

Tiny checking out some late arrivals on Wauregan Reservoir in Danielson, CT, USA.

Another alternative method:

If a dog is only slightly distracted by the trigger, only occasionally whines, and does so with lack luster enthusiasm, I might try using a learned cue to interrupt the behavior. Dogs and horses react well to this technique if they are not fully invested in the unwanted behavior. I might try this if the dog, say, only whines one out of every 8 times passing a trigger.

My Grandmother used to use the word Aaaaaaatttt. I like to use the word woooooop just because I can say it with less effort and it seems to come out sharper and louder for me.

When an animal is only half-heartedly misbehaving I can sometimes sharply and loudly say a word like this to distract the animal from what it's doing; it works like flipping a switch in the animals mind, giving me a very brief few seconds to redirect the animal's attention to something else. Before doing this, I have in mind what I will do to distract the dog because I will only have seconds to initiate it after loudly saying the cue word. This will not work if the animal has an established pattern of whining at every person/dog it sees or it is real intense in its behavior towards the person/dog on shore.

I caution you to not distract the animal for the entire time that the trigger is in sight because in doing that you are avoiding addressing the issue, not fixing it. Use the interrupter cue and redirect the dogs attention to something other than the trigger and then let the dog carry on and see what it does next….see if it goes back to whining at the trigger or if it moves onto doing something else.

Again, what I'd use as a distraction would be based on my training experience, how much distraction I thought the animal needed, and the specific situation I found us in. A chew stick is probably a reasonable option in most cases; the dog is still aware of the trigger, but it's busying itself with a distraction and it can choose how much attention it would like to give to both. The purpose of the distraction, in this case the chew, is not to totally block out the trigger. The idea behind this is to give the dog something to occupy it that will calm it down in the presence of the trigger. The dog can still see the trigger and choose to engage with it; we're just trying to help it make the choice we want it to make.

If you pass a trigger and the dog whines, you use the interrupter cue, and give a chew too many times, you can create an expectation of reward for whining at the person/dog. You can create an established behavior pattern: see trigger, whine, interrupter cue, receive a reward; so don't repeat this over and over again! Be careful not to over use this method. It's only meant to be done on rare occasions, not over and over again. If you do this and the dog goes right back to whining at the trigger, you need to initiate another form of training, such as, what I presented previously in this section.

You can reinforce this technique by training the dog to look at you when you say this cue. I reinforce the wooooop cue with my horse whenever I'm outside doing yard work. For example, I would stop raking leaves and yell out whooop; if his head came up and looked at me, I would walk over and pet him or scratch his withers and other times I'd offer a treat. If he ignored me, I'd go back to raking leaves. I do something similar at the dog park with our dogs. Doing this gets the animal to better focus on me when I use it as an interrupter cue.

The key to successful training is knowledge, patience, time, and understanding.

WHINING WITHOUT AN APPARENT TRIGGER:

I want to be clear that I'm going to be discussing dogs that whine and not dogs that are in a state of panic, aggressive, and/or overwhelmed, and I'm assuming that dog owners should, and would, know the difference. If you're new to dog ownership, not an adult, and/or otherwise not absolutely sure of this difference, please seek help from a professional dog trainer before continuing.

Whining without a trigger is a more generalized whining with no apparent trigger; you can't seem to put your finger on exactly what is causing the dog to whine. It doesn't mean that there isn't a trigger, it just means it's not obvious or there are several triggers overlapping. This usually builds up over time and is an established part of a dogs behavior by the time the owner recognizes the need to deal with it. If you find yourself in this situation, don't blame yourself! Issues like this sneak up on all of us and none of us are perfect; and once again I'll say that our dogs don't expect us to be perfect!

If you're allowing the dog to decide when it wants to enter the kayak as was suggested in the training process, you shouldn't have a dog that whines immediately after entering the kayak at the boat launch. If you do, allow the dog to decide if it wants to stay in or get out. Create a lesson right there at the launch; one that is similar to the introductions you did on your front lawn with the kayak and your dog. Only paddle away from the launch area when the dog enters on its own and is settled.

If the dog immediately starts whining when you leave the launch area and it isn't hungry and doesn't need to pee, poop, drink, etc and its not overwhelmed, then it would be reasonable to think the dog might be uncertain, or even afraid of the new situation it has found itself in. If this behavior is normal for this dog, then you might rationally think it's probably not the kayak or being on the water that is causing the behavior. If this behavior is not normal for this dog, it doesn't automatically mean that the dog can't over-come this and stop whining; it just means that it might not happen during its first trip on the water.

In this situation, I might try to ease the pressure on the dog by not paddling. Don't think because you're in a boat that you have to be moving about. I would allow the dog to position itself wherever it felt most comfortable and safe as long as I thought it was safe to let it do so.

Sometimes dogs that are initially unsure on the water react well to having a light doggy shirt or sweat shirt put on under the life jacket. They find it somehow comforting. Similar to putting a sweater on a dog in a thunder storm.

Whatever you do decide to do, do not coddle a whining dog because you will inadvertently encourage it to whine more. Allow your dog to own their experience; let them work it out for themselves, with as little guidance and reassurance as possible when the dog is whining. Conversely, offer praise and encouragement whenever the dog is not whining and it is behaving as you would like.

Also resist taking the dog out of the kayak every time it whines. Doing that once won't be an issue, but doing it a few times will encourage the dog to whine more. Those of you who have raised children know that if you consistently pick a baby up the instant the child starts crying, and do that every time the child cries, he/she will likely cry a lot more because they are immediately getting what they want when they cry. This is very similar to what can happen with a whining dog.

The dog will think, I whined and they took me out the last three times, so I should whine to tell them I want out now. If you've done this a few times, and then you don't take the dog out, it might whine louder and harder because it believes it's telling you to take it out and you're not listening; the dog is thinking, whining worked the last three times so why aren't you listening this time! It's important to realize that in these situations the dog doesn't view itself as whining inappropriately; it views itself as saying something that you or other humans have validated as a form of communication! The dog sees it as an established form of inter-species communication that is now, from their perspective, being ignored, so they whine more and louder.

If you remove a dog for whining, back up in the process and start over at a point where the dog is relaxed and participating without whining; don't bring the dog back into the kayak until you're quite certain it's not going to whine. If you can't reach this point on your own, get help from a competent professional dog trainer who will come out to the site and assist you.

If the dog doesn't initially whine, but starts to whine say 15 minutes into the trip, then next trip you could back up the process by only staying out 8 - 10 minutes. After doing a few shorter 8 - 10 minute trips, you could start extending the trips in small increments, and only retreating to a shorter time frame if you notice the dog's whining seems to be returning. You could do 2 short sessions in one day if you're planning to be at the location for other reasons throughout the day; for example, you're camping, or at a family event... By doing this, your respecting your dogs level of ability without overwhelming the dog.

Sometimes all that is needed to stop the unwanted behavior is to realize why its happening and to then change the situation or take a step back in the process. For those of you with children or who have raised children, think back to when your son or daughter was a baby; when they cried, you had to sometimes play detective and figure out why they were crying. The reason for the crying determined your next course of action. Its very similar when dealing with a whining dog.

Considering the dog's normal reaction to new things is important; It shouldn't be expected that the dog will react differently to kayaking than it does to other new situations; a dog that whines when its introduced to something new or somewhat stimulating on dry land is probably going to whine when its initially introduced to kayaking; a dog that begs and jumps around on shore will likely beg and jump in the boat. Dogs that get out more and experience more variety should be expected to initially do better kayaking and have a jump on more sheltered unsocialized dogs. However, this is a gap that can be closed with time, patience, and understanding.

If the dog has repeatedly gotten what it wants by whining in the past, it would be inappropriate to think that the dog should act differently in the kayak. This situation can only be addressed if this is changed throughout the dog's life on water and on land. This is usually a difficult task because all people that interact with the dog on a regular basis will need to stop encouraging the whining by not giving the dog what it wants when it whines. This might mean initially out waiting the dog for long periods of time and selecting the appropriate times to do it. I advise you to seek help from a professional dog trainer.

It's a tough thing to accept, but sometimes it's the owner who is unknowingly encouraging the whining! For example, giving too much attention to a dog that is only slightly and appropriately nervous will likely encourage the dog to increase the level of negative behavior to get even more attention.

For example, if our dog, Tiny, started whimpering and shaking because he felt cold and I put on his coat, quickly pet his head, and started paddling again, he'd stop these behaviors and be just fine. If in that same situation, I were to say, "OMG my poor Tine Tine, you're sooooo cold," and cuddle him up to me and cover him with my coat and hold him---what do you think he's going to do? You got it! He's going to shake more because oh boy shaking got him a whole lot of attention. He's going to also think to try it out again when he'd like a wee bit of attention at some other place and time.

If you come to realize you've been causing your dog to whine or whine more, don't be hard on yourself and understand that none of us are perfect and our dogs don't expect us to be!

It's important to not overwhelm a dog. I usually take our dog out on trips that are 3-4 hours or less because he's a small older dog with lots of energy. I'm not rigid about this; sometimes we go over and sometimes under. I try to break up the longer trips with walks on shore. Dogs love to explore new places and these little trips ashore can be just what your dog needs to go on those longer trips. I've occasionally taken him on day trips that had some stops for walks on shore and he did fine. Working up to longer trips is better than tossing the dog into a situation where it has to sit still for longer lengths of time.

If these steps don't reduce or eliminate the whining, I would suggest re-assessing the dog and the situation, and also what the paddler might be doing to cause or reinforce the behavior, paying attention to things like waves, jet skis, motor boats, impending storm, unusual noises... Is it the dog's meal time? Does it need to pee, etc? Ask your friend(s) for their honest opinion and ask friends and people who will give you their honest opinion, not those friends that will tell you what they think you want to hear! If you don't know anyone like this, contact a local competent professional dog trainer to come out and view your specific situation and offer onsite advice.

Asking someone to watch your training sessions can be very helpful because they see all of what is happening. I video record many of my training sessions with animals for this reason. I scan through and watch them later and see things that I didn't recognize while being in the midst of the training session. If you have a camera and tripod, this is a great learning tool for trainers and handlers of all levels and abilities.

In conclusion: *The whiner*

Dogs in general like to be with us and I believe that if the dog understands what's expected and what is going to happen in the kayak, most dogs will want to go, just like most dogs love to ride in cars. As a puppy, our German Shepherd used to puke whenever she rode in my truck. She loves riding in trucks now. It really boils down to how much time and effort we, the owner, want to put into including the dog in our activities when there is a negative issue to overcome.

A final thought on this topic: It is extremely important to exist in the moment when teaching animals. It's unfair to be teaching an animal while your mind is wandering, wondering what you're going to do next or worrying about when you will be able to pay some bill etc; we should never expect from the animal what we are not willing to give them. That includes our full attention. If we expect the animal to give us their full attention, we should in turn be giving them ours!

Animals will not trust us more than we trust them; if you're unsure of what you're doing in the kayak and you add your dog to the situation, the dog will sense your apprehension and no matter how much you try to reassure it, your apprehension is how the dog will gauge it's own level of trust regarding the situation and you. If you're having fun and you're confident about what you're doing, its very likely that soon your dog will be having fun with you!

Tiny on deck at "The Bog."

Communication goes both ways

It's beneficial to learn how animals communicate with each other within their species because certain things will generally mean the same thing from animal to animal across a species. However, please understand that a dog's "standard" behaviors can change when humans are added to the equation!

A pet dog is constantly learning about our language and behaviors and adapting too! When a dog exists in the world of humans, realize that some of the pet's standard behaviors will change as the animal becomes aclimated to its environment; it doesn't enter the human environment and remain stagnant without change! The dog is trying to develop ways to communicate with us while we are trying to learn how to communicate with it.

For example, our dog, Tiny, will bow over and over if he sees the kayaking equipment being moved because he wants to go kayaking. He will do the same if he sees food or a treat he wants or if he wants to get on my lap while I'm at the computer. He has learned that this behavior will tell me that he wants something. He has also learned and accepts that I can say yes or no to what he wants. But, put him into a pack of dogs, and he's not going to do his cute little bow, crossing both front feet at the ankles to tell them he wants something.

This behavior is a form of inter-species communication and a direct result of the dog experiencing ongoing human interactions and being born of a mother who interacted with humans; this isn't pack behavior, nor is it normal behavior for its species until it is brought into the world of humans. This is part of a socialized pet's existence that is not considered within dog training methodologies like "pack leader training."

Here is another example with my horse: When the vet shows up with the ever feared shot, my horse will repeatedly give me kisses because it's trying to gently say take that shot and go away. My horse does this kissing behavior because I taught him the give kisses trick whenever I left. Over time, and with continued reinforcement of the behavior, he has associated giving kisses with my leaving and uses it in the shot situation to gently say go and take that shot with you. My horse has several modes of communication that have resulted from reinforcement of certain behaviors over time that would not be present in a herd of horses. The result is cross-species mode of communication understood by both myself and my horse.

While you're trying to learn to communicate with an animal, it isn't sitting there stagnant like a rock in a creek; it's figuring out how it can also adjust its own communication skills and behavior to help you understand it better! Even wild animals do this. So when thinking about animals within the world of humans, we have to consider how the human element alters the animal's natural communication process.

There are a few good books out there that explain what it means when your dog does this or that behavior and reading those books would be helpful to your training experience. Also consider studying how pets communicate across species because this could better help you understand how your dog is trying to adapt and communicate with you.

Reflections

There is a saying which I heard a lot as a kid. I don't know who first said it; but it went something like this, *You don't get the horse you want, you get the horse you need.* This saying can very easily be applied to dogs as well. A dog or horse will reflect the areas in which a person could improve upon themselves because, to varying degrees, these pets mirror the people around them. For example, if your pet dog or horse intimidates you, look to your human interactions and see that your experiences are really not that different there; you probably don't willingly put yourself into many situations where you need to strongly promote your position to other people who might challenge it! If your dog doesn't seem to *ever listen* to you, your kids probably give you issues regarding this as well. Look within yourself before reflecting outward to your pet!

Trust and Respect

Trust and true *respect* comes with TIME and from understanding and encouraging animals to learn to behave in a manner that is acceptable to us. BUT, THIS TAKES TIME!

Consider this: if a young child is taken out in a kayak and the child doesn't understand that they need to sit still, hopefully, the adult won't be overly dominant and intimidate the child until the child sits still. Hopefully, the adult also won't act or behave like the child to get the child to sit still. No, unless it's absolutely necessary from a safety stand-point, they would, most likely, get the child to sit reasonably still so that everyone is safe and then look for opportunities to encourage the child to *learn,* over an appropriate span of time, that they are expected to sit still even more. <u>We do this because we care about the child and also understand that the child *can't think and process at our same level.*</u> THIS IS SHOWING "RESPECT!" Please show similar "respect" for a dog and your dog will "respect" you more!

If it's not an emergency situation which requires immediate and strong action, don't take all the fun out of the situation! Gradually work toward the behaviors you want from your pet if it's not a safety issue that needs to be addressed ASAP! If it is a safety issue, please realize that not all safety issues need immediate short-term resolution; sometimes an immediate quick and even stern action followed by long-term gradual adjustment is what is best for an animal. In a world of quick fix mentality, this doesn't often happen.

If you are dealing with an aggressive, questionable, or dangerous animal, do not do this on your own. Immediately find a trainer who can help you and don't simply settle on the first one! If your gut tells you that the trainer isn't offering what you think is best, move on to another trainer! A good trainer knows many different styles and methods of training and can blend them together to suit you and your dog's individual needs! There is no one method fits all!

Consider this

I might take some heat for this; but, I'm going to say it anyway. Some modern trainers suggest that we should *pretend* to be a pack leader; they claim that the pack mentality is what is passed down generation after generation and it is what the pet dog understands best. Consider this, the mother dog winces away from a human hand or allows a trusted hand to touch her pup and starts the process of teaching the pup to interact with humans. How to interact among humans is passed down generation after generation from mother to pup; the pups also learn from, and with, the humans around them. Would we *pretend* to be a gang leader to teach even the wildest child to live in our home? Should we *pretend* to be a pack leader to train a socialized pet living in our home?

IF YOU'RE TRAINING YOUR PET WHILE PRETENDING TO BE SOMETHING YOU ARE NOT, YOUR PET IS NOT LEARNING TO INTERACT WITH YOU! IT'S LEARNING TO INTERACT WITH WHO YOU ARE PRETENDING TO BE!

In Conclusion

All that said, there is NO one training method that fits every dog, handler, and situation!! Sorry, it's just not that simple. The various training methods out there have different aspects to them that are helpful in different situations. To train effectively, trainers and owners must learn as much about all of them as possible and be able to use whatever aspect of each is needed at any given time! Every trainer and method of training can teach us something, even if that's only what not to do!

Even if you're planning to have a trainer work with your dog, and you're not planning to do the training yourself, I suggest that you learn as much as you can about the different training techniques so that you'll know if you're being snookered! I once listened to a horse *"trainer"* say complete gibberish, mixing up the trainers that she was quoting and misquoting, and the professional/non-trainer listening to her didn't know that the *trainer* had no clue what she was talking about! The alleged "trainer" was tossing out well-known trainers' names that sounded good unless you knew that trainer X said it, and not trainer B, and the methodology was butchered beyond recognition to someone who actually knew something about the topic. Protect yourself and your pet by learning about the different training methods before hiring a trainer!

BE YOURSELF! Avoid training methods which require that you pretend to be something other than yourself or you're told to hide your habits, emotions, and true self from your socialized pet dog. If you're training your pet while pretending to be something that you're not, your pet is not learning to interact with you! It's learning to interact with who you are pretending to be!

We are emotional creatures and we need to show appropriate emotions to socialized pets during training and when interacting with them. It's more than a little naïve and arrogant to believe a human can hide all emotion from a intuitive dog; nobody has that good a poker face!

If we try to hide and hold back appropriate emotions, what happens if we are in a car accident or we flip our kayak and we're in a momentary state of flux and our emotions can't be held back. In situations like these, we need to instruct the dog even though it's not possible to hide all of our emotions! Don't experience this for the first time in an emergency situation; if you're living in a way that shows the pet the honest and true you, emotions coming out in an emergency shouldn't be a big issue!

This doesn't mean dribble all your emotions out to your dog like they're your counselor. It only means let them see the real you. There are real life advantages to doing this. For example, a pet dog owner who is overly timid and doesn't pretend to be fearless is likely to find that the socialized pet dog with the right personality characteristics will step up and try to protect them in an emergency because the dog sees that as their mirroring role in the relationship. This is affected by the animals personality traits and its upbringing just as it would be with humans.

Learning to communicate with a socialized pet dog is no more difficult than learning how to communicate with a very young child who understands another language and is from another culture! Being patient, deliberate in your actions, observant, fun, and DEDICATING TIME to the process are key to success! Trust and respect take time.

Tiny on deck at The Bog, riding into the sunset on a cool fall evening.

8 TIPS & INSPIRATION

Tiny on deck on the river (under the Rte 395 over-pass) in Griswold, Connecticut, USA.

TIPS

- **UNIQUE DOG CARRY METHOD:** I would not recommend doing the following dog-carry method during your dog's initial introduction to kayaking; however, this information might be helpful to you later on. In situations where it's not easy for the dog to enter the kayak on it's own, I pick our small dog up by the handle on the life jacket and carry him when I'm getting in and out of my kayak. The jacket actually supports and more evenly covers more of the dog's belly area than the dog being carried over an arm and I can balance and maneuver better doing it this way. The jacket has a large Velcro area and two clipped straps to also support doing this and my dog has never shown even the slightest concern over being carried into and out of the kayak this way. And it always brings about a few chuckles from by-standers.

- **WHEN YOUR DOG FALLS IN**, and it will, don't make a big deal about it and don't coddle the dog. Try to act like it's just a normal everyday occurrence. Bring the dog back into the boat, dry them off, and be on your way. If they look cold, put a jacket on them or wrap them in a towel on your lap for a few minutes. Chuckle over it and pet them a little; but, keep in mind that offering too much sympathy and over coddling a dog in this situation can make it more difficult for the dog to get past the experience and deal with the next instance in a positive manner.

- **DON'T BE FOOLED:** There are many different ways of getting training results and varying levels of quality and lasting benefit within those results. Be leery of your dependency on a trainer. The following issue is seen in both horse and dog training realms. The trainer *"trains"* the animal to stop the unacceptable behavior and then shows the owner the changed beast. The owner takes the animal home and over a short period of time the animal reverts back to its old ways and it needs a *follow-up* with the trainer! This creates a nice continuing cycle of pay checks delivered by the owner's feeling of guilt; the owner feels that they have failed the animal because they could not maintain the behavior! B... Hooey! The trainer most likely didn't show the owner what was actually required to keep the animal behaving in the expected manner, knowing a return visit would be likely to occur. This also frequently happens when intimidation and/or force is used and the animal returns to an environment where the owners don't use force and/or intimidation. So before you bring a dog to a trainer, insist that you are able to watch ALL of the training sessions. This will allow you to see all of what was done with the animal and what you need to do to continue the behavior at home. If you don't understand something ask because you're paying for the dog to behave outside the training situation, not just in the presence of the trainer. Don't drop your dog off and leave. If you bring your dog home from a trainer and its behaving oh so wonderful and then the dog reverts back to its old behavior more than 2x, find another trainer! Don't go back to the same one! They're likely more interested in your wallet than you and your dog. A good trainer will observe owner and animal and choose a training method that the owner can follow up and use at home even if that method is not the trainer's favorite form of training!! Yes, competent trainers should know and be able to use more than one method of training! A good trainer will clearly show you what you need to do to continue the behavior and should have no problem allowing you to watch and even participate in the training sessions.

- **FLAT WATER RIVER TRIPS** are fun situations to include dogs. However, unlike being in a pond or lake, turning back on a river can mean hours of paddling to avoid paddling the longer distance forward if your dog starts acting up. Breaking up the trip with a few stops along the way goes a long way towards keeping your dog satisfied with a longer river ride. Dogs naturally love to explore and the change from sitting still to walking and romping really benefits the dog. I stop, get out, and walk Tiny about once every 1 - 1 1/2 hours when I'm on flat water river trips with him. We have found some interesting animals, birds, old foundations, stone structures, paths and so forth on these mini breaks from paddling too. I also occasionally stop and let him jump off the deck and go pee while I sit in the kayak and wait; I do this using a retractable leash. This gives the dog a few minute break from being on bored. I bring a chew or a stuffed Kong toy because these items can be taken out and given to the dog if they seem to be bored with a section of the river. My dog is seldom bored, but has on occasion appreciated the Kong or chew being in the pack.

- **NO-SEW HOMEMADE DOGGIE SWEAT SHIRTS** are great for kayaking dogs because you don't have to worry about your dog ruining any of its good clothes! If you have a dog that is Tiny's size you can use the sleeves from your spouse, boyfriend, friend, or son's sweat shirts to make them. Just use a sweat shirt that, oh let's say, got eel all over it and it didn't come out in the wash--with a few snips of the scissor it becomes a thrifty no-care shirt for your kayaking dog. The shirt is worn under the life jacket so it won't be visible to people inter-acting with you and your dog. 2x or larger is best for a dog Tiny's size; the one in the photo is made from the sleeve of a 1x men's sweat shirt and it's a little snug. The cuff which becomes the neck band can be left up like in the photo, or turned down. Cut the leg and pee area holes and then put it on the dog and snip a hole for the harness clasp. Be sure you leave ample room for the legs and that it's not pinching underneath. The material won't unravel through many washings so there is no need to sew or hem it. I cut them a couple of inches from the tail area because he needs ample pee space underneath; if you cut that much away underneath and leave the top to the tail, I find it tends to flop around more than I like.

Cut leg, pee area, and harness clip holes, being certain that leg holes are not too tight.

When cutting the leg holes, start small & low and recheck as you make the holes bigger.

- **A FIND-ME-BELL** attached to the dog's life jacket can be helpful if your dog gets away from you and is trotting through the woods ignoring your calls. You can stop and listen for the jingle and know which direction to look. You can get these at many discount stores for only a dollar or two. You can even use a Christmas ornament bell. Hold it loosely in your hand while you walk around the store and move it around to make sure it's only going to make noise if the dog is jogging along and not every time the dog turns its head. A nice loud jingle is best.

DOG PARKS, HIKING TRAILS, AND OTHER POINTS of interest for your dog can be researched online before visiting new kayaking locations outside your immediate area. I supply this information on my website for Connecticut because I like to bring our dogs to a variety of different dog parks and hiking trails because I know they enjoy these activities. What dog doesn't enjoy a romp at a dog park! Imagine your dog's surprise when it gets to go kayaking and then visit a new dog park or trail! I make sure to park in the most visible and most accessed portion of the parking area and I lock my kayak into my truck when I'm at these secondary locations *(see next tip below for details)*.

- **WHEN LOCKING MY KAYAK IN MY TRUCK IN A PUBLIC PLACE** *(like the ones mentioned above)*, I use a heavy cable lock (not a bike lock/cable!); of course, anyone driving around with heavy-duty bolt cutters can cut the cable, but the average impulse thief is not likely to leave the area, hunt down bolt cutters, and return to steal it. They will generally move onto an easier target unless that is the very specific item they want. Position the lock/cable as far from the first point of entry as possible to make the cable hard to access without potential thieves making a public scene. If they think people will take notice, they will also be less likely to try to mess with it. Using two cables can also fluster a thief because they want to be in and out quickly and don't like additional surprises. You could also use a heavier chain with a lock; however, I don't recommend doing this because, if you do this a lot, a chain constantly being dragged against your kayak as you put it on and take it off can tear up the finish on your kayak. Attaching something that makes noise to the cable(s) is also a good deterrent; a nice item for this is a cow bell! It's hard to get off and will make quite a racket; put the bell on the cable in a spot that is farthest away from the point of entry where its difficult to get at it, but, so that it is loose and will make noise when the cable is moved. When my kayak is in the back of my truck with the cap on, I sometimes back up to a wall or building if possible because if the kayak is all the way in the bed of the truck with tip of the kayak almost touching a solid object like a wall, there is no room to get it out without removing the truck cap. I have also backed up to the side of a friends vehicle and done the same thing. These are things I do or have done; it's up to you do decide what you think is safe and best for you in the situations that you find yourself.

- **EXPERIENCE THE EMERGENCY BEFORE THE EMERGENCY:** Before you bring a dog in a kayak with you, go to a local swimming area with a friend and enter the water with your life jacket on. Float and move about with it on so that you know what it feels like and how to move about with it on before you have an emergency situation. No need to go out over your head. Pretend to move an item about as if it were your dog in an emergency situation; then with your friend spotting you, do this with your dog, if you feel confident that it would be safe to do so. With an experienced professional kayaker, tip your kayak and learn how to right your kayak and get back in. Ask them to show you what to do if you have a dog with you. Have the instructor show you the proper procedures for preventing your kayak from flipping. There are two paddle maneuvers (an upper paddle position and a lower paddle position) that can in many cases stop you from flipping when your kayak has reached its furthest balancing point. Know these! Make sure you get a professional to help you with this!!

- **KAYAKING GROUPS:** There are a few local small groups in my area that post online and on "meet up" to let people know that they are getting together for a kayak outing and inviting new people to come along. There might be similar groups in your area as well. I caution you to bring friends AND DON'T GO ALONE if you don't personally know members of online groups, don't meet in private places if you choose to participate. I belong to two local online groups and one national group that hold local outings in my area. I personally prefer to be a participating member of a local group rather than joining a group on "meet up" where the members might change week to week. Again, I'm just tossing this information out there, but you need to decide what is right, best, and safe for you and your dog.

- **CREATING A SCRAP BOOK OR PHOTO BOOK** might seem like a silly suggestion; but many people will say, "yes, it's a good idea," and then not follow through and actually do it. I suggest that you do it so that when you and/or your dog are older and can no longer paddle, you can look back and recall the adventures. Photos will bring back experiences your mind stored away and might not readily recall without them. A hard copy or computer generated scrap book or photo book can also, on your passing, become a treasured item of your children and grandchildren as they recall Grandma's or Grandpa's adventures with Fido! Don't cheat them of this pleasure--make the scrap book! One of them might even be inspired to write about your adventures!

- **EARRINGS:** If you're a woman, don't wear big earrings or earrings with loops when kayaking with a dog. I learned this early on when I was a teen. When you're interacting with a dog in close quarters, like you would in a kayak, the dog can very easily get a nail stuck in your earring and rip it out of your ear! OUCH!

- **COLD EARS!** Tiny likes his sock hats *(next photo)*! I cut out the sole of the sock, leaving enough space at the toe to cover the ears and enough of the band to go around the neck--then slit the rest of the sock in ½ up the back of the sock. When the sock is slipped over the dog's head, the toe goes over the ears, the face looks out from the open hole in the sole area and the lowest part of the sock band goes around the dog's neck with the remainder of the sock spread out flat under the dog's sweater and/or life jacket. Neat colored cheap socks can be purchased at local discount stores. I like to use solid colors, like bright orange or green, because he would be better seen in an emergency if I had to look for him. This is great if an unexpected wind picks up or your pet is out on the water in the crisp autumn air. They can more easily be chilled in these situations because they are sitting or standing still and not being active and generating heat.

Tiny on deck & dressed for the crisp Autumn breeze at Roseland Pond in South Woodstock, Connecticut, USA.

Tiny on deck on the Quinebaug River near Canterbury Bridge.

SOME INSPIRATIONAL THOUGHTS

Negativity can suck your enthusiasm out of your dreams and ambitions faster than your vacuum cleaner can suck dog hair up from your floor! Don't let the negative words of others keep you from doing safe, fun, and exciting activities with your dog.

For example, I put my kayak onto a very shallow small pond near our home one evening; I wanted to watch Tiny experience different types of carpet on the deck of my kayak before picking one to line the deck. I had stopped at Dunkin on the way and filled my coffee cup, and Tiny and I were floating around on the pond. It was a warm day and the breeze lightly carried my kayak across the tiny pond, and then without much effort, I would dip-paddle back to the other side and once again float back towards the ramp. Tiny fell asleep on deck so I left him sleeping while I finished my coffee and enjoyed the sunshine.

I hadn't paid much attention to the people on shore until a lady turned and looked right at me and said, "What kind of person doesn't know any better than to take a dog out in a kayak!"

I almost laughed, not due to what she said, but because her sharp words woke my sleeping dog with such a start--and the look he gave her was priceless. My moment of chuckle gave me a few seconds to consider my answer. I told her, "I guess, the same kind of person who didn't know any better than to teach her horse to throw a partially deflated basket ball and play catch!"

"Hummph." was all she said.

Her negative words did suck a little joy out of those few moments, but we moved on, floating about and enjoying the afternoon. We watched people come and go; some played with dogs and some fished.

Then as we were making our way to the boat launch, a lady said to her husband,

"OMG! Look she has a dog in that kayak! This is great! Look..." She was tugging on his arm and experiencing true excitement; her enthusiasm was matched only by my own.

My point is that you're going to meet people who don't like what you do and you're going to meet people who like what you do. Don't let the one's that are negative about what you're doing bring you down! As long as the activity is legal and safe for all involved, and you and your dog are having fun.....well, isn't that what it's all about!

Regardless of the activity, if you're interested in doing something, learn about it. Being informed about what you're doing can, and will, really boost your confidence. If you like kayaking, but you don't know much about it, challenge yourself to learn at least one new thing before you go out on the water next time. And make it a habit to learn something new between every paddling trip. I read articles, blogs, and posts on the internet and watch videos and talk with people about kayaking on a regular basis.

Many times, it is the people who are new to kayaking that teach me something that I didn't previously know; this sometimes happens because people tend to pay more attention to the details of a situation when the experiences are new to them. For example, a person experiencing a river for the first time will likely notice more intricate details than a person who has paddled that river many times throughout their lifetime. A more inexperienced child will tend to notice even more. People generally stop paying close attention to things they frequently see and experience on a regular basis. So someone new to kayaking will likely pay more attention to the more intricate details that I've grown accustomed to and view as every day occurrences.

Keep in mind too, that even if you're not a professional, and you know something about kayaking, you know more than someone who knows nothing about it. You have the ability to help someone that knows less than you and helping such a person is a great way for you to learn more too! If you keep learning and doing, before you know it, you'll be helping others learn how to kayak with their dogs!

Don't be intimidated by the fact that you're not an experienced dog trainer or you're not a professional paddler. Maybe you've never trained a dog; doesn't matter! If this is you, you have an advantage over people who are experienced trainers and professional paddlers! *<u>While it's extremely important to know the basics and the things that could be a danger to you if you don't know them</u>*, the upside to not believing you *"know it all"* is that you're not set in your ways when it comes to brainstorming solutions and new training techniques. You will also have a more open mind when someone makes a suggestion that is a little different from something you might normally try. There is always more to learn!

When I was very young, my Dad would sometimes take us to visit our cousins on Sunday afternoons. One of my cousins had a cat that he had trained to drink milk through one of those silly crazy straws that were common place back in the 60's. Oooops, just gave away my age again. When I saw that cat suck milk up through that twisted plastic straw, I was inspired to think that I could teach animals to do just about everything! My imagination just exploded with ideas!

Imagine what my life with animals would have been like if I had not witnessed my cousin teaching that cat to suck milk out of that silly straw. I would have grown up and likely learned all the traditional means of training animals and perhaps not given other more unconventional methods a second thought. Fortunately, my first experience was way outside the norm and, going forward, my problem solving generally was too. Many times w-a-y outside! LOL!

People who have learned something, anything, to a point that *they believe* they know most of what is available for them to know within their field, will generally no longer look outside the norm for alternative solutions. They will most often look to tried and true methods that have proven themselves in the past. People who are new to doing a particular activity are the ones who will generally have a more open mind and come up with some creative solutions. So don't sell yourself short because you're not an expert. I never want to reach a point where *I consider myself* to be an expert because that would mean I would stop trying to find new ways to do things!

Tiny on deck watching fish jump at Williams Lake in Lebanon, Connecticut, USA.

Kayaking has mental health benefits. I can't tell you how many times different people have told me that there isn't as much exercise involved in kayaking as there is in other sports and outdoor activities. I tell them, it's not about the exercise! It's about how much my brain unwinds and how much I let go of all that holds me back! I absorb the thrill and the beauty around me and recharge! Exercise, whatever the amount, is just a side benefit. However, I will say that if you find an activity, like kayaking, that you're passionate about and you enjoy doing, you will most likely stick with it more so than an exercise routine that has little long-lasting draw to it.

One of the neat things about kayaking is that it's very easy to find others interested in kayaking. All you need to do is load up your kayak and equipment, go to a large body of water with public boat launch access, unload your kayak, and paddle it! I write about my kayaking experiences and I do kayaking and hiking site reviews on my blog, KayakingCTwithLou.com, and so I'm often saying, "Hi. Hey, what fish have you caught?" or some other conversation opener. Paddlers in general are very friendly and easy going. Some prefer to be left to themselves, but most will at least say hi and smile before paddling on. Some will stop and chat.

I hope you've enjoyed my book. There are some resources in the next chapter and I've included Tiny's favorite dog biscuit recipe.

Your feedback is valuable and important to me! If you liked my book, please take a few moments to write a positive review for my book on the site in which you purchased it. Your show of support would let others know this book is a good read and help promote my book. Promoting my book would allow me to spend more "work" time writing more books. I would greatly appreciate your show of support. Thanx again. See you on the water!

9 RESOURCES

WEBSITE: KayakingCTwithLou.com

- *It's A Dog's Life* is the part of our website dedicated to dogs. This section includes information related to kayaking, hiking, dog parks, and how to information.
  http://kayakingctwithlou.com/category/its-a-dogs-life/

- Visit our website at KayakingCTwithLou.com and subscribe to receive updates, including site information and notifications regarding new books and videos.

- *Life Saver* is a part of our website where you'll find our Newsletter Archive, information for beginners, and things like how to request a site review.
  http://kayakingctwithlou.com/category/lifesaver/

YOU TUBE CHANNEL: KayakingCTwithLou

Supplemental video "Kayaking CT: Paddling with a Dog" You Tube address:
HTTPS://WWW.YOUTUBE.COM/WATCH?V=M79JKNDS3EI&LIST=UUICIEWKHZELGG-QFKEZDKOG
If you watch this video and find it helpful, please give us a thumbs up! Thank you.

- Kayaking and hiking site reviews for CT area also available on our You Tube channel.

- Subscribe to our You Tube channel, KayakingCTwithLou and keep up to date on all the new upcoming kayaking and dog training videos.

EMAIL: KayakingCTwithLou@paddlingCT.com

I would like to hear from you! Have an idea or a book topic that would be of interest to you, let me know! Have a question, ask! I will try to answer as many questions and help as many people as time will permit.

If you found this book to be helpful and you're feeling generous, please write a good review on the site where it was purchased to help support and promote the sale of my book and to keep more books coming! Thank you for choosing my book.

Above all else, a valued pet and cherished companion.
A well behaved dog comes with knowledge, time, patience, and understanding.

Billings Lake, North Stonington, Connecticut, USA.

RECIPE: TINY'S FAV DOG BISCUIT

1 c rolled oats
1/3 c margarine
1 c boiling water
3/4 c cornmeal
2 teas sugar
2 teas beef bullion
1/2 c milk
1 c shredded cheddar cheese
1 egg beaten
3 c whole wheat flour

Preheat oven to 325 degrees.

Mix rolled oats, margarine, bouillon into boiling water and let stand 10 minutes. Add milk. Then thoroughly stir in corn meal, sugar, cheddar, and egg. Mix in flour a little at a time until stiff dough has formed.

Knead, mixing in more flour until dough is smooth and no longer sticky.

Roll out dough on a lightly floured surface to about 1/2" thick.

Using cookie cutters of a similar size to each other, cut out biscuits and place them on a cookie sheet that has been covered with parchment paper. You can place them relatively close together because they don't expand much in size. I also re-roll dough scraps that are left after cutting biscuits and cut more biscuits from it.

Bake 35-45 minutes in pre-heated oven or until golden brown and cool. Store in loosely covered container in refrigerator.

ABOUT THE AUTHOR

Lou Racine is a blogger who shares her kayaking experiences and writes kayaking and hiking site reviews on her website KayakingCTwithLou.com. Paddling since childhood, she continues to paddle one to three times a week, weather and time permitting. It is a common occurrence to see their dog, Tiny, sporting his orange life jacket and lounging on the deck of her kayak.

Her love for animals was strongly influenced by her father and grandparents at a very young age. Attending her first official dog training classes with her grandmother and their two dogs, she learned the Koehler dog training method. Her grandfather introduced her to horses and her father & grandfather encouraged her to communicate with animals in ways that weren't currently being publicly explored and accepted.

Growing up she was involved in camping, kayaking, hiking, hunting, trapping, fishing, target shooting, horse back riding, and other outdoor activities. She attended, and graduated from, a local trade school where she studied automotive repair. Spending significant time in Vermont during those years, she developed a strong desire to one day hike the Appalachian Trail; it's one of two items on her bucket list.

Living in Connecticut (USA) all her life, she later traveled with her son to many parts of the country. Their quest to visit every state tragically ended more than ½ way to their goal when her son passed in a car accident in 2000.

She holds an AS in Human Services with honors from QVCTC in Danielson, Connecticut, USA. Preceding her son's fatal accident, she was working on her BS and she spent much of her time helping children. She worked as an aide in the SPEARS program in the Putnam Middle School, supervised and coordinated an after school and summer youth program at TEEG in North Grosvenordale, tutored privately and in the Learning Lab at the college, and advocated for the children she tutored. She drew young people into everything that she did. For example, in her role as campaign manager for a local state senator, she was often accompanied by a group of students who volunteered and helped throughout the campaign. She received the 1998-1999 Youth Volunteer Award for her efforts to involve youth in community activities.

Her son's passing caused her to withdraw from these community activities. Lou hopes to re-ignite her passion for helping children through her life-long love of writing in the near future.

Manufactured by Amazon.ca
Bolton, ON

32170098R00044